ROCK YOUR GIG and GET PROMOTED
by Rich McDonald

First edition

Praise for ROCK YOUR GIG and GET PROMOTED

"Rich's application of Jesus' teaching— 'Think of others before yourself' —is a pretty rebellious way of looking at business. Rock on Rich and keep playing that Fender."

Alice Cooper, Rock Legend

"Richard has written a truly insightful book based on a lifetime of career success. I thoroughly recommend Richard's book to those if who strive to realize their full potential."

Andy Mooney, CEO Fender Musical Instruments Corporation

"Rich was there for me as a colleague & trusted advisor back in 2002 during an unexpected, but much needed reinvention in my own life. He was a real mentor to me, as he continues to be throughout this book. His wisdom and life experiences come through loud and clear across these pages. Musician or not, this is a must-read book for everyone about the "gig" of life!"

David Ellefson, Bassist / Co-founder of MEGADETH

"Inspiring, eye-opening and maybe the most important book you'll read."

John 5, Rock Artist

"*Rock Your Gig and Get Promoted* was so informative my highlighter almost ran out of fluorescent ink... This book is the perfect intersection of a story, textbook and self reflection tool that was truly refreshing to read."

Brad Howard, CEO Trend Nation

"When you think of your favorite music, you're thinking of a team with good chemistry. A team, a group, or a gang, which is what the Alice Cooper group felt like, at it's best, is firing on all cylinders because of the practices Richard spells out so clearly in this book. We couldn't explain it back then. We listened to each other's ideas, voted on the best one, and followed whatever path pointed to achieving our collective vision. And we willingly evolved with the growth of that vision.

When young musicians ask me what it takes to make it, I suggest reading this book, it hits home."

Dennis Dunaway, Alice Cooper group

ABOUT THE AUTHOR

Rich McDonald is a successful business advisor, career coach, author and keynote speaker. His passion and expertise is sharing the inspiration, perspectives and tools that contributed to his many personal and professional accomplishments.

Prior to establishing the BOOST211 Consulting Group, Rich served as the Executive Vice President and Chief Product Strategist of Fender Musical Instruments Corp. His celebrated, twenty-five year career with the iconic American brand began with an entry level position and progressed to include numerous global leadership roles.

His accomplishments include philanthropic service as the founding President of the Fender Play Foundation, and board member of the esteemed National Association of Music Merchants. Rich's accolades include the prestigious Music & Sound Retailer Lifetime Achievement Award and Hall of Fame inductee.

ACKNOWLEDGEMENTS

If you want to go fast, go alone.
If you want to go far, go together.

African Proverb

Rock Your Gig wasn't a solo walk through the desert, I didn't make the trip alone, I had talented help guiding me along the way. I'd like to acknowledge the tribe that took this incredible journey with me, and made this book a reality.

I have to start by thanking my amazing wife Lisa. You created the space and environment for me to write this book, proofed every page, offered valuable insight and kept me believing. Thanks honey, this would not have happened without you.

Micah and Charlee, thank you for understanding how important this book was for me. Your support, enthusiasm and interest energized and inspired me.

Rich Siegle my creative partner and coconspirator. Thank you for believing in me—yet again. Your passion for the subject, tireless creative energy, hours of design and layout, all made my words come to life—thanks buddy.

Rachelle Marmor, my Business Manager and long-time friend. Once again, thank you for your guidance, input and support—and encouraging me to write in English! Your input was vital.

Thank You All,

Rich

FORWARD:
ASTRAL WEEKS

I've known Rich McDonald for about a third of my life. We've been collaborative co-workers, band mates and tennis partners. Our mode of operation has always been dynamic, fast-moving and competitive, but always in a harmonic and creative context that resulted in extremely rewarding experiences. When Rich announced his retirement awhile back, I was happy for him, but it felt like the end of something.

It was avery reflective moment for me (naturally an even deeper one for Rich), because I knew I wasn't far behind. But it felt very uplifting despite the circumstances—uplifting because we had traveled very different life paths and yet, because of our shared passion for music, those paths had magically crossed and we were both better off for it. You see, music has a tendency to turn normal co-working relationships into life-long friendships—actually "family" is a probably a better description.

One day, a text came through, "Hey! I'm writing a book! Want to help with the design?" So much for retirement. As I always have, I said , "Sure!" Like every other project we've shouldered together, this one would take us both into uncharted waters, but we had some pretty strong navigational tools at our disposal—our collective experience.

Rock Your Gig, takes some tried and true practices and reimagines them. One of the breakthrough moments came when we were discussing the graphic representation of the *Personality Designs* four square matrix. Traditionally, it's depicted as four boxes; but putting people into boxes did not line up with Rich's view of reinvention and understanding others. His vision is something more fluid, more interactive and more harmonious (yeah, like music). We hit upon a different symbol; a möbius strip. What's a möbius strip? Pretty simple, it's somewhat like a figure eight, with a bit optical illusion thrown in. But there's no smoke and mirrors: you can actually construct a möbius strip with a piece of paper and a little tape. What you get is a perpetual motion device—an endless loop that takes you in, out, over and under. It also looks and feels like four distinct parts all streaming into each other.

Now we were getting somewhere—four distinct personalities, but not in boxes. Instead, they form an organic structure where all four live, move and interact along a co-dependent course. It's a beautiful symbol for the concept, idealized for sure, but that's the goal; motion, balance and harmony in pursuit of a better, more successful "you".

Let's make a möbius strip. You need a standard 8 1/5 x 11" sheet of paper, some scissors, a pen and a little piece of tape. Take the sheet of paper and cut a 1" strip off the long (11") edge. Take pen and draw a line right down the center length of both sides. Now take the two ends and bring them together. Before you tape, turn one edge over, and then apply the tape. You have just made a möbius strip! Hold it with two hands by the outer edges and twist it ever so slightly in opposite directions to achieve the figure eight effect. Now follow the drawn lines—they no longer stop at the paper's edge. They don't begin and they don't end. Twist it around—it can take on a triangular shape as well. A little artsy-craftsy, a little "Whoa!", but you now have an appreciation for the elemental symbol within *Rock Your Gig* in all its magical, three-dimensional glory—one that the printed, 2D graphics on the following pages can never quite achieve.

It's a trippy little thing—it describes motion, ebb and flow, tension and composure, speed and relaxation. Think about it as you take Rich's *Rock Your Gig* journey. It's a path that leads into undiscovered territory, but always comes back to you.

– Rich Siegle

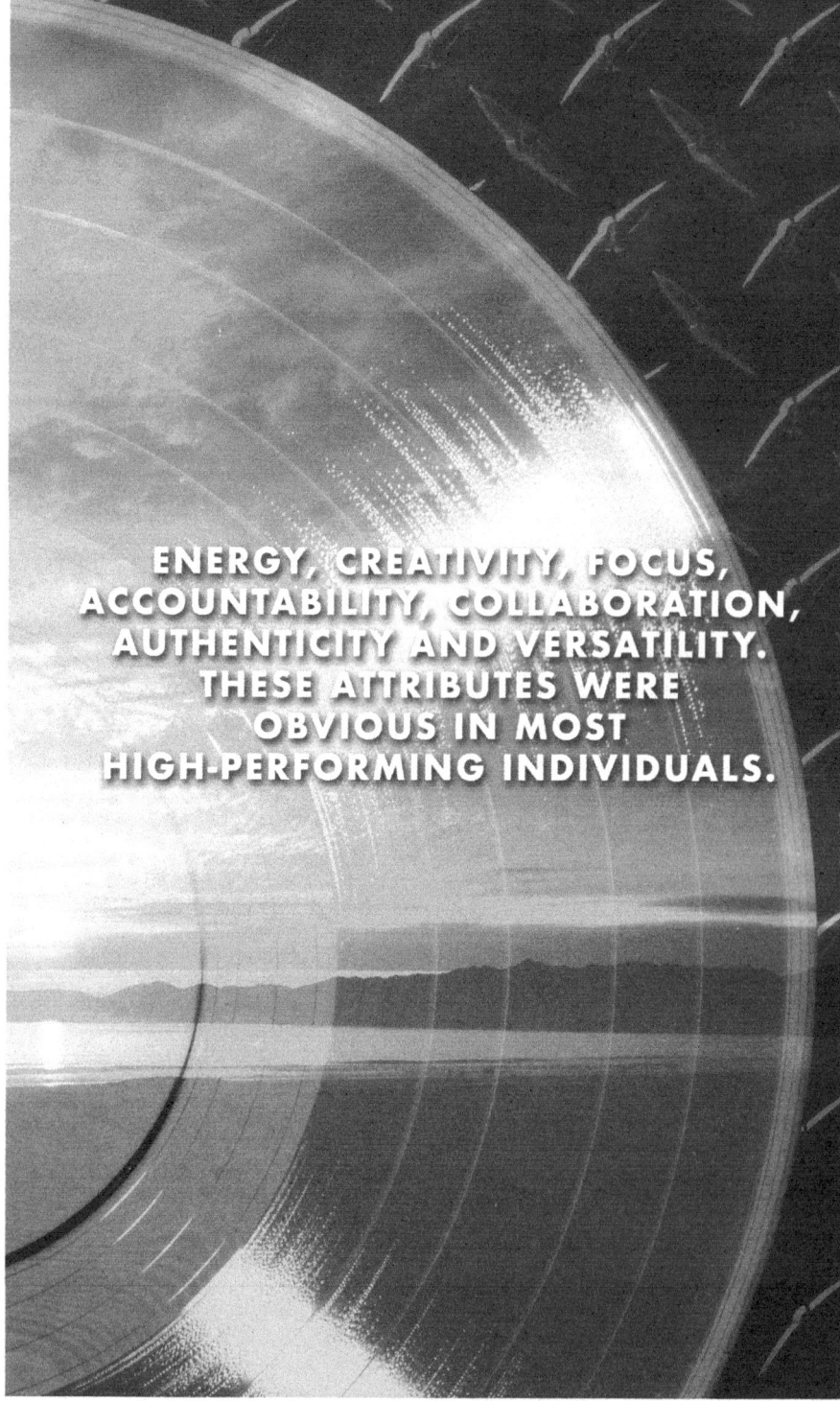

ENERGY, CREATIVITY, FOCUS,
ACCOUNTABILITY, COLLABORATION,
AUTHENTICITY AND VERSATILITY.
THESE ATTRIBUTES WERE
OBVIOUS IN MOST
HIGH-PERFORMING INDIVIDUALS.

ROCK YOUR GIG and GET PROMOTED
RICH McDONALD

INTRODUCTION:

REFLECTION

The genesis of *Rock Your Gig* was reflection. Not the casual "what did I have for lunch yesterday" reflection. I'm talking about a deep, thoughtful, post-mortem type of reflection—the forensic retrospective that only happens at the big intersections in life. Graduation, your daughter's wedding, the passing of a loved one, or the passing of time; those stop-drop-and-recollect moments when you try to take it all in and answer the burning questions—what just happened and how did I get here?

In my case, the intersection was retirement. The specific catalyst, my yet-to-be-penned retirement speech. An amazing twenty-five-year career at Fender Musical Instruments was coming to an end. It had been nothing short of a dream-come-true for a guitar-crazy kid from Scottsdale, Arizona. Now, it was time to synthesize this incredible journey into some salient perspectives to deliver from the podium. Of course, the primary objective was to try not to bore the heck out of everyone waiting to get to the hospitality bar and keep from crying if at all possible.

So, I sat, pen in hand, familiar Moleskine journal at the ready ...reflecting. Even in the midst of this technological word processing tsunami, I still prefer the tactile partnership of a Moleskine journal. They aren't made with mole skin, are they? I sincerely hope not. Sorry, I digress.

Poised to begin, I pondered. There were the requisite questions that needed to be answered; "What were my proudest moments in product development?", "Who were the coolest artists to work with?" I looked over my shoulder at this dynamic, diverse experience searching for the answers to these questions and others. What were the standout cap-stone memories? What defined the value and essence of my career, from the inside out? How did I end up where I did?

I rummaged through the past; the innovative, award-winning products that changed the way musicians create, share and curate their music, the disruptive business strategies that propelled Fender into a leadership role in the rapidly evolving retail landscape, the globalization of Fender's Marketing and Artist Relations divisions, the awards and accolades—both professional and personal—none of them really rose up in the mix. Honestly, not what I was expecting.

The first synthesized perspective to surface was privilege. It accurately captured so much of what I was feeling. Privileged to steward a legendary brand that I absolutely adore, privileged to have my fingerprints on its iconic products, privileged for the creative freedom, trust and support I was given.

The sense of privilege was quickly followed by a feeling of gratitude. I couldn't be more grateful for the opportunities my career at Fender had afforded me. When I joined, the brand was barely on its feet after suffering a long decline at the hands of former owner, CBS (yep, the television and music conglomerate). It was a small, scrappy, passionate team that was engineering the turnaround. Your job description was "Whatever needs to be done" which created a broad scope of opportunities, if you were willing to step up.

It dawned on me how powerful of a motivator desire can be. There were challenging times for sure, but I never had to discipline myself to get up and go to work. Desire beats discipline in the long run I told myself. I was grateful.

So, it wasn't specifically the product or the artists, it wasn't the world travel or the disruptive business strategies. Yet it was all of that. What was missing was the common denominator. The thread that ran through all those bucket list experiences. Then it occurred to me (even as self-absorbed as I can be) that, rising through the mist of all my memories, were people. Lots and lots of people—the many wacky, talented, passionate individuals I worked with across every division, in every corner of the world. My memories shifted from individuals to the teams they made up. It makes me smile to recall the crazy, cool, unexpected outcomes that occurred when passion and diversity are focused on a common goal.

Countless key strategies created by teams big and small; digital engineering teams, sales teams, marketing teams, artist relations teams, trade-show teams, operations teams, budgeting teams, forecasting teams, customer service teams. Intellectual property teams, "You are being deposed, we are here to prep you" teams, culture team, holiday party team-people and teams are what really defined my career.

A wave of relief came over me. My retirement speech suddenly had form and dimension. I felt privileged and grateful to serve a brand I had loved since I was a teenager. What stands out in my mind's eye are all the amazing people I worked with and the teams we served. I imagined I would probably have to say a little more to get the nice watch (I jest), but it was a sincere, authentic perspective on my career that I could honestly share.

The retirement events went off without a hitch. Yes, event(s), there were two. One in the Fender Hollywood office and one at the Scottsdale campus. I was terrified that I would be an emotional wreck. As it turned out, everyone else was and, by the time I took the stage, all the tears had been shed. I have never felt as professionally honored, respected and appreciated as I did during those events. Indeed, in my world, it really was about people and teams.

As the weeks passed, as I acclimated to life without the yoke of employment, I kept thinking about the people and the team dynamics I experienced in my time at Fender. I couldn't stop thinking about it. You get such a unique perspective when you come into leadership as I had done—the long way, from the ground floor. You have a sense for what it's like on both sides of the fence.

Like a relentless studio producer, I listened to the sessions over and over in my mind. Who was a little off the groove on this track and what players are sitting pretty in the mix? What songs were doomed from the onset and why couldn't we see the inherent flaws? I loaded the deck with my career compilation reel and gave it a listen.

For years I was getting promoted and I really couldn't tell you exactly how or why. I started in an entry level position in Fender's Customer Service department taking calls for replacement parts. I'd see the ten-digit part numbers in my dreams—0064063000: reverb tanks Twin Reverb amp. I was promoted ten times in twenty years, eventually becoming Fender's Executive Vice President and Chief Product Officer. It felt like I was motoring along, working hard like everyone else and, suddenly, like an alien abduction without all the creepy medical stuff, I was picked up and dropped into a new role. I never felt ready, I was always scared I was in over my head—and it always turned out well. Or as Michael (one of my favorite Artist Relations reps) told me, "Dude, what a mic drop career!" Why? What was I doing differently than my peers? What did I have in common with other successful executives?

At this point I was absolutely captivated and driven to understand more about human connectivity and team dynamics. Research, case studies, interviews and personal peer reviews all came together organically in the months following my retirement epiphany. That's what it looks like when desire is driving! My father once told me, "If you really want to learn about something, find a way to fall in love with it." I was falling in love with understanding the mechanics of personal and professional fulfillment.

I searched for the consistent traits running through the undercurrents of all these positive, elevated careers. I was looking for *Patterns of Success* which are defined as, "...the consistent behaviors, attitudes and beliefs that define our personal and professional profile." Essentially, the positive things we do that contribute to our success. I formalized my approach and started building a "data cube" of sorts to keep track of the variables.

Energy, Creativity, Focus, Accountability, Collaboration, Authenticity and *Versatility*—these attributes were obvious in most high-performing individuals. I'm generalizing for sure, it's very situational and role dependent, but overall these traits are table-stakes and shared by most motivated individuals. Here is where it got interesting; possessing all these attributes did not guarantee success, or even stack the deck in their favor. There were many individuals that possessed most, or all these traits yet failed to secure trust, happiness and success. What was missing?

My perspectives started taking shape when I backed up from the individual's profile to examine the team dynamic. How did these high performing individuals navigate the team environment? The assumption is easy: energized, accountable individuals with high integrity working together equals a bad ass team. Right? No. Sorry. This was the moment *Rock Your Gig* came to life.

I started to see the universal nature of individual and team success. The successful, fulfilled peers I observed in my corporate career shared the same foundational magic as those from my musical sphere. It didn't matter if they were a bass player in a ska band or an analyst in the finance division, their long-term success shared a similar motif. It was clear to me at this point. Individuals, teams and businesses, just like bands, sustain a higher level of personal and professional fulfillment because they were able to leverage these two powerful concepts.

Interpersonal Awareness

The first thread of commonality was only visible, measurable and real when these individuals were interacting with others. The magic was in the effectiveness of their connectivity. They possessed all the necessary attributes, but they also had what my mother called, "people skills." They possessed the power of interpersonal awareness and made efforts to understand others; they were effective communicators and great listeners. Their peers wanted to see them win. Not because they were overtly qualified, but because their peer group appreciated the way they connected with them.

These successful, evolving performers were all Gig Rockers: they proactively extended themselves beyond their default comfort zones to generate positive interpersonal connections. When you are onstage with musicians that listen as much as they play, special things happen. The same forces are at work in business. If you want to *Rock Your Gig*, you need to be in-tune, in-touch and in-the-groove. You need to be willing to "take it to the bridge" like James Brown, change it up, step out and jam.

The Spirit of Reinvention

The second trait was much harder to identify as it required long term observation. The individuals sustaining the highest levels of performance over time—and I mean decades in some cases—were those demonstrating the versatility, willingness and desire to reinvent, to evolve—to step through the doorways of professional maturity (or just maturity for that matter), manifest fresh capabilities, reenergize, learn and grow.

The same parallels to artists and bands remains. Those that evolve, sustain relevance with their audience and positively navigate the band/team dynamic rock-on for what feels like an eternity (think Rolling Stones, Rush, AC/DC).

These two material conclusions—the power of interpersonal effectiveness and the capacity for reinvention—form the foundation of the *Rock Your Gig* philosophy. In the pages ahead, I will share perspectives from my observations and research, offer you tools and the inspiration you need to take a new purposeful approach to career success to *Rock your Gig and Get Promoted*.

REINVENTION IS PROACTIVE
IN NATURE AND ENRICHES
THE FIELD OF OPPORTUNITY

CHAPTER 1

THE SPIRIT
OF
REINVENTION

CHAPTER 1.

THE SPIRIT OF REINVENTION

Newness and Renewal

Consider for a moment, the power of "new." Refreshed, reimagined and re-energized "newness" feeds our core. On a universal level, it's part of the natural cycle of renewal – the shedding of the old to accommodate the new. It occurs on a molecular level within all living things and, on the macro level, driving the planet's global biome. It's everywhere.

New home, new cars, new phones, new attitudes, new information, new software update (not again!), new financing terms, new extended warranty, new cures for old problems – captivating, powerful, *new*. In a world of calculated Search Engine Optimization (SEO) strategies, *new* is still one of the most powerful words in advertising.

If reinvention and newness are part of the universal fabric of life, and a good thing—why don't more people do it? There are a million variables (and even more excuses) that can keep us from tackling reinvention. One reason is, we don't see the need for it. We will discuss this more in upcoming chapters, but the bottom line is this: we lack the self-awareness to see any need to reinvent, evolve or grow. We do, however, see all these needs in others. How convenient. To add a twist of irony, we pretty much all believe we are in touch, in tune, actualized, masters of "self". Indeed, ignorance is bliss!

A Plan

Interestingly, businesses are far more likely to reinvent than individuals. Businesses have something we typically don't —*a plan*. The processes used to define growth include the evaluation of established beliefs. The first step in recurring strategic planning is the postmortem. As the name suggests, its objective is to evaluate performance to expectations or to a plan that has run its course. Not just a look back at what happened, but more importantly, was the belief system that formed the foundation for these goals on target? We believe, therefore we develop plan X—we measure, adjust as needed, rinse and repeat. Can you imagine if you had a plan, a personal roadmap for your life and you were reviewing it on a regular basis? What would be different?

Reinvention is a solution. It's not change for change's sake. We reinvent to solve a personal issue, to start fresh, to elevate performance, to sustain relevance, create new opportunities, to grow and evolve.

The comfort and illusion of security keeps many of us locked in the status quo.

For many of us, sameness creates comfort and security. It completely contradicts the progressive nature of life, but it's the human condition to seek a safe routine. A false sense of security keeps people and businesses from stepping out into the unknown or up to the next level. Consider Kodak, the revered and legendary photography brand that gave us "Kodak Moments." They invented the digital camera in 1975[1], granted it only captured black and white images at a resolution of .01 megapixel, but they had the future in hand. Kodak couldn't reinvent itself from a chemical company to a digital photography house in time to seize the opportunity. What were they holding on to and where is it now?

We want thing to improve but we don't like the idea of changing anything.

When is it time to reinvent? There are those disastrous episodes in life that scream for reinvention. Please, for the love of God! It's usually pretty obvious to everyone around us and eventually it lands painfully in our lap. Time for change. That may be your situation. Your marriage is struggling or, worse, has ended, your career path is unstable, you may be distancing yourself from addiction or recovering from cancer treatment. These are all powerful catalysts for personal reinvention and they are all circumstances that I can relate to because I experienced each of them.

Your world doesn't need to be collapsing around you to feel the Spirit of Reinvention tapping you on the shoulder. I can recall sitting in the conference room at Fender as a young-manager level employee. I had recently been promoted and was sitting up to the table with senior level leaders for the first time. It didn't take long for me to size up the competition and realize I was in trouble. My enthusiasm, creativity, passion and guitar playing may have earned me a seat at the table, but it wasn't going to keep me there.

Every time I reached into my bag of business chops it was painfully empty. I would rummage through it under the table, looking for perspectives to offer while the conversation rapidly moved along without me.

I was in my 40s with a high school diploma and very little corporate anything. "Maybe I should reinvent, elevate, catch up", I told myself. I enrolled in night school and pounded out a Bachelor of Science in Business Management. I went to school for years to finish the degree, but the experience started paying dividends immediately. It may not have been apparent in my high-level contribution, but it was energizing and inspiring me. I felt the progression and my esteem was elevated. I was on a journey of reinvention.

Adaptation vs. Purposeful Reinvention

There is a line between adaptation and reinvention. Adaptation is reactive in nature and more about survival than growth.

Reinvention is proactive in nature and enriches the field of opportunity. Both require change. Both require us to drop old perspectives and behaviors and adopt new ones. If we find it difficult to adapt to change in general, we will struggle when called to reinvent.

When is reinvention the right solution? When we consider true "gig rockers", they all seem to be in a state of readiness and possess a willingness and ability to adapt to new situations. They have a sense of self, so they know where they are starting from and have the versatility to make adjustments. They adapt and reinvent in a continuous cycle.

The more visible, classic reinvention often corresponds with a new job, a promotion, marital status change, geographic changes, health challenges or many other variables. These intersections all create dynamic opportunities to take a new approach, to reimagine, to reinvent.

A Personal Continuum

The need for reinvention, like many things, occurs across a continuum. There can be dramatic circumstances in life tailor made for reinvention—times when you just want to look in the mirror and see someone different staring back. If you're standing at one of those big life intersections, a total makeover may be the remedy. Even as dynamic and wacky as my life has been, I have only had a couple big bridges to build that required significant personal or professional reinvention. Those moments usually come crashing down on us with a bang, or a loud sucking sound. It doesn't require your radar sensitivity to be high—it's a clear, absolute, obvious need.

Gig Rockers

Gig Rockers possess something different. They carry the *Spirit of Reinvention* with them everywhere. You see the evidence in their curiosity and open-minded approach. They display a willingness to consider new points of view and a willingness to challenge their own beliefs. They seek the feedback of others and never become comfortable in the status quo. They are in a perpetual state of readiness to leverage change.

Once again, we can learn from high-performing businesses and apply their strategies and processes to our personal and professional evolution. The Toyota Production System was created by engineer Taiichi Ohno[2] between 1948 and 1975. The system revolutionized manufacturing and gave us principles such as JIT (Just In Time delivery), Hoshin (creating a line of sight throughout the enterprise) and Kaizen. Kaizen is a system of interconnected processes created to drive continuous improvement. It is based on the idea that small, ongoing positive changes can drive meaningful improvements. In general, it is based on cooperation and commitment and stands in contrast to approaches that use radical changes or top-down edicts to achieve transformation.

The *Spirit of Reinvention* is the principal of Kaizen applied to our lives-continuous self-evaluation fueling a cycle of improvement. We are entities that strive for efficiency, productivity and profitability. And, since we are human, we can also add happiness, fulfillment and success. It all starts with a willingness to change and a desire to grow.

REWIND: SPIRIT OF REINVENTION

Reinvention:

Reinvention can be challenging because...

1. We lack the self-awareness to see the need for change.

2. We feel safe in the status quo.

3. There is no mechanic at work in our lives to stimulate growth.

Reinvention is the willingness and desire to evolve. It is evident in individuals sustaining the highest levels of performance over time and is demonstrated in their versatility.

Reinvention inspires, energizes and elevates businesses, teams and individuals.

Newness and Renewal: (page 20)Newness is captivating and drives demand. New is still one of the most powerful words in advertising. Renewal is a natural cycle at work in the universe, dismantling the old to accommodate the new.

A Plan: (page 20)

Businesses are more likely to reinvent than individuals. Strategic planning requires a business to evaluate its performance against a set of beliefs. Individuals can profit from this practice.

Adaptation vs. Purposeful Reinvention: (page 22)

Adaptation is reactive, purposeful reinvention is proactive.

A Personal Continuum: (page 23)

Reinvention occurs on a continuum. There are radical opportunities that require courageous change and subtle opportunities for refinement.

Gig Rockers: (page 23)

Gig Rockers carry the *Spirit of Reinvention* with them everywhere. You see the evidence in their curiosity and open-minded approach. They display a willingness to consider new points of view and a willingness to challenge their own beliefs. They seek the feedback of others and never become comfortable in the status quo. They are in a perpetual state of readiness to leverage change.

CHAPTER 2

SITUATIONAL ANALYSIS

CHAPTER 2.

SITUATIONAL ANALYSIS

Let's talk about designing great balance and harmony within the ecosystem of "you." Perhaps you're thinking, "What is this New Age mumbo jumbo?" Let me be a little more specific, the ecosystem of "you" is just a metaphor for the functionality of your life; you, your physical, emotional and spiritual selves and the external world around you. "You mean my life is like a fish tank and I'm a fish? Or maybe a turtle?" Well yes, a very handsome turtle with a truly divine design, spiritual awareness, opposable thumbs and a job. And you know what happens when the fish tank is out of balance? Green, mucky, stinky algae where only those creepy things attached to the glass are happy. "You're scaring me." —Yes, I hope so.

Balance

You may feel skeptical when you hear terms like *Life Balance*, *Laws of Attraction* or the *Power of Positivity*. It's a narrow, knee jerk belief system that may come into play: fear change, hate and criticize things you don't understand, especially when it comes to alternative ideas such as these.

Personally, I always knew positive thinking was powerful, but I didn't really know what it looked like. I think I heard something about balance or harmony in an episode of *Kung Fu* when I was a kid—David Carradine as Kwai Chang Caine, the kick-ass-if-I-have-to mystical philosopher to the '70s baby boomers. I never really had any idea how balance would impact my life, positively or negatively.

If this is an eye-rolling topic, you need to muster up some

open-mindedness and hear me out. This is all absolutely real, universally known, old, old news that is unimaginably powerful yet most of us won't give it a second thought. We may buy in at some level, but not necessarily enough to purposefully pursue a balanced lifestyle. Note, I didn't say, "Achieve a work-life balance.", we will discuss that later in detail. I said, "Pursue a balanced lifestyle." which isn't just offsetting the demands and stress of employment or home. It's about mining the energy that a purposefully balanced personal ecosystem offers. Let me un-package it a little more before I ask for your buy-in. I'm going to take the long way around, so stick with me.

Stress

Our world is evolving at an exponential rate. The complexity staggers the imagination. It's invisible in the moment, it just appears as frenetic energy; the hum and hustle, the rhythm of life, a snapshot of a busy world. But over time, the hum and hustle begin to create fatigue, stress fractures appear, the rhythm of life takes on the annoying cadence of a dripping faucet we can't ignore or fix.

When I consider the fragmentation that has occurred in my lifetime, it's hard to fathom. When I was a kid, the pet food area of the local market was a small portion in the home goods aisle. It was about eight to ten feet long—dog and cat food, litter, some flea collars and tick-dip, the classic hot dog squeaky toy. Today, the pet food aisle is a store, rather several stores, the size of the entire supermarket I just referred to! You can find all your pets' special dietary needs, if, for example, you have a lactose intolerant cat.

This is a whimsical example of the mass fragmentation and specialization in play today but it's also an example of what is happening in almost every facet of our lives; more and more captivating things to consume, more change occurring faster, the rate of obsolescence increasing. Seriously, how many types of toothpaste do we really need? I can feel my stress levels rising as the option anxiety sets in. What does fragmentation and specialization have to do with balance? Everything!

Marketing Mayhem

We are mesmerized by consumption. We cannot get enough of anything. The dumps are full of all the stuff we needed—for a minute. The world keeps fragmenting to keep us interested, to keep us watching, to keep us buying. Businesses need to grow; people need to spend. You don't have the money? No problem, we have you covered...

The biggest marketing con in the history of mankind: turning the absolute slavery of debt into the freedom of credit.

We want more, so we need to earn more, so we work harder—to pay the debt. It's like that 1980s community service ad (maybe before your time) with a stressed-out dude rationalizing, "I do cocaine so I can work harder, so I can earn more money, so I can buy more cocaine, so I can work harder, so I can earn more money." We are the addict, and cheap, disposable goods is our cocaine. Our lives are out of balance. Ironically, we want more and more of what *doesn't* make us happy. Say it out loud, "We want more and more of what *doesn't* make us happy." Our lives are out of balance.

Let's consider the shift in the American workplace over the past fifty years and the resulting lifestyle changes it fostered. In 1970, women made up about 38% of the total labor force[3], by 2015, women represented 46.8%. During that same period the number of working mothers with a child under the age of three increased from 34% to over 63%. Women, and specially mothers, are working in greater numbers, with younger and younger children at home. Greater understanding, empowerment and increasing opportunities for women are also part of these numbers. More women are in the labor force because they can and want to work. That being said, more women are working because they have to, as well.

As the number of working mothers with young children increases, the number of working fathers with expanding roles in the home increases. Everyone is working harder. Again, our lives are slipping out of balance.

The average American earns an annual salary of $56,515 and carries debt of $38,000 not including home loans[4]. 69% of college graduates in 2015 took out student loans, the average amount was $29,800. Of that number, 14% of their parents borrowed another $35,000[5]. We often start our adult lives in debt up to our eyes and seemingly do everything we can to increase its hold on us. Simply put, our lives are out of balance and it is negatively impacting the health of our personal ecosystem.

The picture is similar when when we take a look at our health. It is estimated that 35% of American adults are dangerously obese[6]. We are the global leader in big and tall, except we aren't tall. The CDC tells us the number of diabetics has risen to 9.45% of the population. Another 84.1 million of us are pre-diabetic. If left untreated, we will become type-2 within five years. Our houses are bigger, our cars are bigger, our plates are bigger, our Big Gulp sodas are bigger and, subsequently, our butts and stomachs are bigger. And we are sick. Our lives are out of balance.

"There is more to life than increasing its speed." – Mahatma Gandhi

We have to snap out of it-unplug like Keanu Reeves in *The Matrix*[7]. We need to wake up and start seeing things for what they are and what they are doing to us. At the very least, we need to ask a lot more questions. Why are we so obese? Because we eat too much bad stuff and sit down. We are in *The Matrix* and don't even see it. Drive down a central retail corridor and count the fast food restaurants. Count the fast food restaurants that focus on meat and sugar. Look at the billboards, what are they selling? Watch the Tostitos Fiesta Bowl and have a chip.

But wait! The FDA is here to save us, right? You're not obese, you're big-boned! You can be diabetic and live a perfectly normal life, we have a fix. Do your knees hurt? We have a pill and a procedure for that too. High blood pressure, low blood pressure, "just right" blood pressure? We can fix that too! Baby, don't you worry your sweet little head, Big Pharma is here to enable every self-destructive behavior you can come up with.

Of course, we can 3-D print you a new liver, do you want a beer while I'm up? You have insurance, right?

In 2017 the CDC (Centers for Disease Control and Prevention, isn't it funny that they left the "P" out of their acronym?) published reports on America's opioid epidemic[8].

- Healthcare providers (our doctors) wrote *241 million* prescriptions for opioids. 66.5% of America has received an "OK for heroin" note from their doctor.

- More than 11 million people abused prescription opioids in 2016 alone.

- Over 1,000 people a day end up in emergency rooms from opioid abuse.

- As many as 1 in 5 American's received long-term opioid prescriptions for non-cancer related pain in the primary care setting.

- The CDC estimates the total economic burden from prescription opioids, is an unimaginable and staggering $78.5 billion annually.

What happened? How did we get obese, addicted, unhealthy and in debt up to our double chins? How did this become our status quo?

Surgery to remove a stage-3 cancerous tumor in the left-occipital area of my brain earned me a backstage pass to "The Greatest Show on Earth" (that's an old travelling circus slogan), and the second greatest marketing scheme in the history of mankind. You wonder how we got here. What happened? How did we become pill popping, unquestioning healthcare lemmings? Doctors aren't evil (at least the ones I have met). In my experience, they have been passionate, caring individuals. I think their hearts are exactly where we all would want and expect them to be. The human race has just never liked to ask too many questions of sages. Questions like, "Where did these big pharmaceutical companies come from?" What role did they play in my doctor's education? Is there any connection between my congressman, the FDA and these really, really, really big drug companies like Phizer, Johnson & Johnson, Rosche VI and Bayer? Speaking of Bayer—didn't they have to testify at the Nuremberg War Crimes Trials[9] as part of I. G. Pharma Ltd. for using forced labor to produce pharmaceuticals in the largest factory in the world? I believe it was somewhere near Auschwitz, Germany.

You mean Bayer, the aspirin company? Yes, they trademarked acetylsalicylic acid as Aspirin in 1899. The previous year, they trademarked heroin (yes heroin, junk, smack, black tar, horse, white lady) for use as a children's cough remedy—with "No side effects!" Heroin[10]? Isn't that an opioid? The more things change, the more they stay the same.

Proactive Curiosity

Please start asking more questions. Become curious about your world, your health, your food. What triggered the explosion of the pharmaceutical industry? Innovation. Scientists working day and night to find cures for mankind's most debilitating diseases. I'm sure there was some of that Louis Pasteur vibe, but what really made it happen was this:

The identification of "Disease" as a marketplace, and the government support of genetic patents.

I am not asking you to believe anything you have just read. My mission isn't to convince you Big Pharma is out of control, I'm not a conspiracy theorist and I'm not asking you to be one. I am asking you to be a little more curious, more aware and more accountable than I was before a life-and-death experience woke me up. You don't need traumatic experience to start seeing a less distorted, less manipulated view of your world and how it impacts the ecosystem of "you."

Over-Consumption

We push more and more onto our plates; not just food but bigger portions of everything. Every week, every day, every hour needs to be filled. Families run themselves ragged chasing after school activities that elevate life skills and enhance our children's lives. Really? Society has told us to keep our kids busy all the time, even if you can't afford it. Our children need to be engaged in activities as much as possible. Really? The typical family today runs a non-stop calendar of extracurricular activities on top of an increasingly demanding school schedule. Our children go to school for just about the equivalent of a workday just like us. Then homework, just like us. Then baseball, basketball, volleyball, soccer, dance, swimming, lacrosse, track and field, karate. These are all awesome life skills for our children, but how much is enough? How much is too much?

Who is raising our kids? Have we relinquished our parenting authority to teachers and coaches because we are too busy to take on the responsibility? Where does rest come into play? When do families regenerate and realign? At the dinner table? What dinner table? It's a grab-and-go lifestyle. Our ecosystem is under siege. Our lives are out of balance.

Why have I dragged you through this seemingly militant point of view about the state of our world today? I'm throwing matches, I'm trying to start a fire. I am trying to find a trigger that will cause you to stop and think about your life in a different, more objective way. To look inward at your mental and physical state and more closely at the environment in which you function, the environment you create and the beliefs driving your behaviors. It's foundational to starting this journey—to elevate and prepare yourself to *Rock Your Gig*.

Presence of Negativity

Rock Your Gig is about harvesting the power of positive connectivity and creating more energized, uplifting interactions with others. It's about enriching your relationships and, consequently, your life, through elevated interpersonal awareness and behaviors. We cannot optimize our interpersonal potential if our ecosystem is under attack and our lives are out of balance.

As our lives stabilize and we begin to seek balance, our ecosystem responds with abundance.

As in nature, when we fall out of balance our ecosystem takes a hit. Why? Because we are part of it, for crying out loud! The same rules apply. Positive energy in, positive energy amplified. Negative input in, negative energy amplified. You are the sun that powers the ecosystem. When you shine bright, you bring illumination, power and warmth. When you turn your light off, you spread darkness, weakness and cold.

I asked myself many times, "Why didn't I see the impact my belief systems were having on my life? Why didn't I think it would change anything? Why did it take something incredibly painful to wake me up?" I'm not a psychologist, maybe you are (and I realize there are many variables in play), but I do know this:

We don't establish value until there is something tangible to compare it to.
We usually don't even know we feel bad ...until we start feeling good!

We don't know what balance will achieve in our lives because we often live in a state of perpetual imbalance. Maybe you have observed this. You drive your car for a year or two and, at some point, you get a flat and you go to the tire shop. You sit in the lobby, notice "tire guys" (that breed of person able to take on the removal and repair of a tire), customers of every type and always those weird automotive magazines you never seem to see anywhere else. An hour-and-a-grand later, you get behind the wheel and drive away. You say to yourself, "Holy cow, it feels like a brand-new car, it's like the whole front end of my car was rebuilt, this is amazing!"

The health of our ecosystem is similar. Like the tires on a car the wear is slow and linear, like the boiling frog. The deterioration is so gradual we don't notice it—until we do. The deteriorating performance becomes the norm, the standard of expectation.

We don't see how rest will change our lives, because we don't rest for any sustained period to see the result. We don't make radical changes to our consumption to find out it's not normal to sit up all night eating Rolaids. We don't meditate because that's for "new-agers", so we never see the powerful impact it can have in our lives. We never hear the words to a love song, until we are heartbroken. It takes faith.

Faith

"You're telling me, the key to a more actualized life and career success is hidden in the lyrics of a post-Wham George Michael song?" Not exactly, but I have to admit, it's a great catch phrase, "You gotta have faith."

It takes faith to build a bridge to a foreign shore, to reach for something in the dark. If you don't believe your life will improve by seeking an elevated level of balance, then it most certainly won't.

Have faith that focusing on the health of the Ecosystem of You will pay dividends. It will do things you expected it would and a whole lot more. Have faith that learning more about the impact of nutrition will lead to a new way of looking at what you consume. Have faith that exercise will reduce your pain and dependence on medications. Have faith that you can step outside the powerful current of social norms, rise above the complacency and status quo and lead your family to higher ground. Believe this is important. Believe it will improve your life. Believe you can do it.

REWIND: SITUATIONAL ANALYSIS

The Ecosystem of "you":

A metaphor for the systems and interdependent functionality of your life—you, your physical, emotional and spiritual selves, and the external world around you.

The ecosystem is an interdependent, dynamic, evolving force. Each element's functionality is dependent on the other. Our physical health is influenced by our emotional health and vice versa.

Balance: (page 28)
The ecosystem is optimized when it is in balance. When in balance, it generates energy and abundance. But balance is not static, our goal is to continually seek it.

Stress: (page 29)
Our world is evolving at an incredible rate. Fragmentation creates greater levels of complexity and increased stress on the ecosystem.

Marketing Mayhem: (page 30)
The two greatest marketing plays of all time: rebranding the slavery of debt as the freedom of credit, and identifying disease as a marketplace.

Proactive Curiosity: (page 33)
Our personal ecosystems are under attack and we don't know it or we choose to ignore it. We need to be more curious about the things that impact the health of our ecosystems; diet, drugs, stress, rest.

We need to be curious about our food, our health, what we believe and why—seek new perspectives, ask questions, be thoughtful.

Over-Consumption: (page 33)
Americans are mesmerized by consumption. We want more of what doesn't make us happy. We want more and more of what we can't afford.

Presence of Negativity: (page 34)
We are numb to the negative patterns and beliefs in our world and our lives.

Faith: (page 36)
Have faith. Believe that a holistic view and purposeful curation of your Ecosystem will elevate your effectiveness, relationships and joy. Believe it matters.

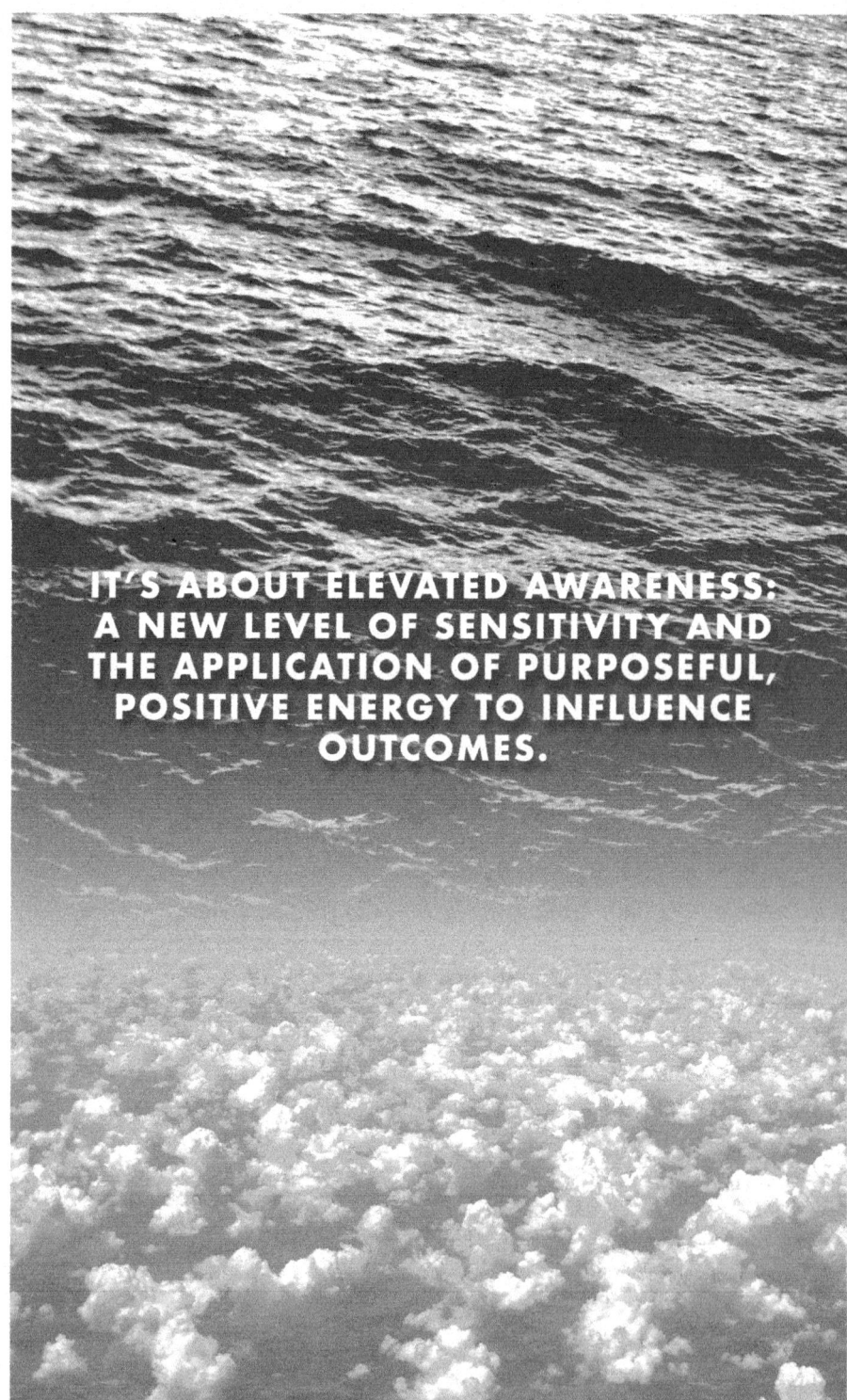

IT'S ABOUT ELEVATED AWARENESS:
A NEW LEVEL OF SENSITIVITY AND
THE APPLICATION OF PURPOSEFUL,
POSITIVE ENERGY TO INFLUENCE
OUTCOMES.

CHAPTER 3

THE
ECOSYSTEM
OF
"YOU"

CHAPTER 3.

THE ECOSYSTEM OF YOU

Rock Your Gig takes a unique look at life balance. There is no shortage of perspectives on the topic and most deal with seven to ten elements of life balance—*Finance, Relationships, Work, Health, Romance* and *Environment*. Yes, these are all great areas to investigate. My problem is, I can't remember ten things! I can get to about six of the really heinous, obvious laws outlined in the ten commandments, but I'll be damned if I can recall them all.

As Gig Rockers, we are interested in a specific outcome; elevated, inspired interpersonal relationships. We want to throw off sparks and create positive connectivity with others. We want to focus on the elements that pay the greatest returns across the broadest scope of applications. We need a perspective that raises our sensitivity and awareness of Balance. The question becomes, "What has positive or, conversely, negative influence on balance?"

My intention is not to offer you some mystical, enlightened view and a detailed roadmap to life balance. First off, it doesn't work like that, and second "I'm not worthy" (in the words of Wayne and Garth bowing before Alice Cooper). It's about elevated awareness: a new level of sensitivity and the application of purposeful, positive energy to influence outcomes. It's about believing something has value, seeing the need, and leaning in on it. You don't need to be a Yoga Master, although you may benefit from a yoga class, ok? You don't need to become a fully actualized Mahavishnu of life balance. I am suggesting that you step back and take an objective look at your life choices. Why are we doing this? Why do we care? Because the healthier and more balanced our personal ecosystem is, the smoother it functions. The smoother it functions, the more abundance it creates. The more abundance it creates, the more growth we experience. We are like radio transmission towers on a clear day: when our personal ecosystem is in balance and healthy, we transmit with incredible energy. Our signals are heard clearly across great distances. Positive, focused energized communication enhances reception. We hear and understand others with greater sensitivity and people receive our transmissions with greater clarity and understanding.

Think about it. How hard is it to bring an energized point of view to a conversation when you feel like a bucket of dirt? How clear is your transmission when you are preoccupied by a failing relationship or even a temporary fight with your spouse? How hard is it to get excited about the potential of your life when you're struggling to understand the meaning of it? We may not be able to see it, but we are affected.

Conversely, what happens to our transmissions when we feel good; when our relationships are empowering us and our life has purpose and direction. We vibrate with a positive energy, our messages become focused, our outlook positive and energized. We see growth, we see blessings and abundance.

THREE DOMAINS OF FOCUS

The *RYG* philosophy focuses on three areas (yes, because I can always remember three);

I. Physical Health

II. Emotional Health

III. Spiritual Health

It's through these lenses that we will evaluate the effectiveness of our interpersonal engagements. These three areas influence the ecosystem in material ways. They have the potential to greatly enhance or undermine our objectives. If they're of the undermining variety, they distort and diminish the effectiveness of our communication. We may be aware this condition exists, and we may not.

Illness, low self-esteem, lack of focus, insomnia, anxiety, pain, hurt and doubt—all of these can be a very obvious negative influence on the health and stability of our ecosystem. Any degree of these mental and physical afflictions can throw us out of balance and diminish our effectiveness.

3a. When Physical, Emotional or Spiritual Health are compromised, we lose energy, clarity and focus. The result is diminished interpersonal effectiveness, weak or distorted negative connectivity.

3b. Physical, Emotional and Spiritual Health sustains our balance and bring energy, clarity and focus to our interpersonal communications. The result is enhanced positive connectivity.

I. PHYSICAL HEALTH

Our physical bodies are the engines driving the turbines that generate and distribute power to the ecosystem. No pressure there. Our physical health plays a role in how much energy we produce, and the quality of that energy. In other words, is it clean (positive) power or dirty (negative) power? Both can drive us, but they go in very different directions. The nature of the ecosystem is inter-dependence. Not only does our physical health influence our attitudes and perspectives, our attitudes and perspectives influence our physical health. This is why we want to take an integrated approach to life balance through the lens of our personal ecosystem-—the ecosystem of "you."

We can have significant health challenges that don't overtly impact the ecosystem, that don't throw us out of balance. We may have learned to navigate, process and minimize some obstacles we've encountered. Or a hangnail could bring us down. For most of us in mid-life or younger, our health is, you know, our health. Until something breaks. But here's the thing, stuff rarely just breaks. It happens, but typically it's part of a much larger problem and can become a linear path to system failure.

The tendency is to ignore, minimize or rationalize the warning signs. "Power through!" was always my philosophy, right up to the day I tipped over. Whoops. Eighteen hours later I was having brain surgery. Which, if you aren't aware, is this interesting mix of medieval medicine and high-tech robotics. They bolt your head into a cage to hold it still. I didn't know that until I found the four holes in my head where they screwed it into my skull. Ok, then.

Even when I really started feeling bad; low, low energy, numbing headaches, stomach jacked-up, I just wrote it off to getting old, being tired. Even as I was laying in the hospital (before they told me I had a "mass"), I was convinced they were going to tell me to lose weight, slow down, exercise—you know, get real about my lifestyle. Nope.

I accomplished a lot on a personal and professional level in a ten -year period. I'm really proud of the legacy my career represents. I did it swimming against the current of my wellness and at a pretty high cost to my young family. I could have accomplished far more, spent more quality time with Lisa and the kids, learned and experienced more, if I had placed greater value on my physical health.

After all the cancer drama, I was able to make the connection between my health and my strategic energy, interpersonal effectiveness and happiness.

The "Ecosystem of Rich" repaired itself, yours will too.

Today, I enjoy all the benefits my physical health offers. I'm in my 60s and healthier and happier than I was in my 40s and 50s. I have more energy driving my intellectual curiosity, elevated awareness and social effectiveness. I feel better and everything works with less friction and fatigue.

We can choose to ignore some of the most basic signs of declining health. We tend to avoid the awkward conversations, they're personal and weird. Sometimes it's so awkward we don't even discuss it with ourselves, denial is the preferred option. Men are famous for pretending they don't have asses.

PHYSICAL HEALTH: Flags We Shouldn't Ignore
• **If you snore.**

Sorry, it's not normal, your wife hates it and can't sleep.

• **If you have insomnia.**

Stress may be working overtime just like you.

• **If you're one-hundred pounds overweight.**

It's probably not genetic, it's food and exercise.

• **If you have high or low blood pressure.**

Do you even know?

• **If you eat a handful of Ibuprofen every day for pain.**
Stop immediately. Consult a specialist.

• **If you have a 32oz soda every day.**

Wait for it, wait for it...

• **If you only have a bowel movement every three days.**

No, that's not normal, normal is two times a day.

• **If you feel tired and you're sure gravity has increased.**

Gravity isn't changing.

• **If you sweat when you eat or look at a stairway.**
Type 2 waiting room is open.

These are all signs we can easily and often do ignore. The bottom line is this: our *Physical Health* matters on so many levels— including the subtle nuances at play in our relationships. Don't choose to ignore the signs. If things are going well, all the better—start elevating your health. Increase your energy output by increasing physical wellness. Exercise, take a walk, lift a few weights, take a swim, stretch, get your blood moving. It doesn't take much to start feeling the benefits. You may have to work through a week or two of discomfort if you have been inactive, so take it slow. But take that first step, then another and another. Walk toward and embrace your physical health and start enjoying the benefits.

II. EMOTIONAL HEALTH

Oh great, "emotions." Ok, you're going to talk about emotions. Hang on, I'll just be a minute. I need to run back to the Bat Cave, I left my... uh, "feelings" thing in there. Go ahead and start without me, no worries, I might be a while. Ok, I'll text you...

Not the easiest topic for some of us. Believe me, I get it. I mean I think I do. At any rate let's pop the top on this one. What do we mean by "emotional health?" In this context, it's about being in a state of awareness with the ability to control and regulate our emotions, feelings, thoughts and behaviors. We need to learn to regulate the appropriateness of emotional responses. It doesn't just mean being "happy", it means we are aware and able to regulate the ebb and flow of a variety of natural emotions to maintain "happy". The goal is to not be victimized by our thoughts and subsequent feelings.

This is another one of those circular conversations that spirals upward. Your emotional health is enhanced by investments in your physical health. You feel energized by the increase in self-esteem. Your A+ attitude drives elevated connectivity. Bridges are built to cross the widest of chasms. Success inspires you to invest more in your physical health. As you do, its positive impact on your emotional health is realized. It's a perpetual engine of wellness.

Much like our physical health, warning signs of our emotional health can be obvious or screaming silently in the undercurrent of our busy lives. Similarly, we can ignore them if we choose... until we can't. Everyone has emotions to deal with, even first officer Mr. Spock demonstrated true emotional caring for Captain Pike in the original pilot of *Star Trek*, "Captain, Jim... please.... don't stop me." You always knew, under his cool exterior, that there were emotions at work below the surface. Yes, even Mr. Spock!

Let's focus on two areas of our emotional health; **Cognative Distortion** and **Self Esteem.** Gig Rockers understand the importance and value of emotional health. They use it as a differentiator, they leverage their versatility and resilience. Their interpersonal intelligence recruits champions to their cause. Once again, we seek enlightened and new arenas of sensitivity. We want this new curiosity to be a catalyst for positive change.

EMOTIONAL HEALTH: Cognative Distortion

Cognitive distortion is all the stuff we tell ourselves in the absence of any real, meaningful and accurate information. Conveniently colored in shades of gray to support every emotional ensemble, our upbringing is often dominated by the word "No". Many of us end up seeing the world as a "glass half empty."

Dr. David Burns, author of *Feeling Good*[46], debunks a common misconception we have about our moods. To us, it feels like we are being victimized by our mood. Our mood is coloring our perspective and making us unhappy. We woke up on the wrong side of the emotional futon. The truth, however, is the opposite! What we think colors and defines our mood. Wait, what... really? Yes indeed.

I don't want to over-simplify, Dr. Burns' book is excellent and if you need a deep dive into emotional dynamics, buy it. I'll do my best to highlight the relevant points for *Rock Your Gig*.

First, we observe and experience events in our world. This input comes in three flavors—positive, neutral and negative.

Next, we process this input via our thoughts. We rewind the movie over and over in a continual cycle which is called our "internal dialogue."

Finally, our feelings (AKA our mood) are created by the output of our thoughts; a. I heard this. b. That means this. c. Now I'm sad. What's amazing is the "That means this." part of the equation—it's usually all jacked up, distorted, improvised, made-up, manufactured and orchestrated by cognitive distortion. Are you getting the picture? We speculate to the negative in the absence of any real information. It's what we do. We can, however, do it less! Look for these pitfalls that Dr. Burns has identified.

• All or Nothing Thinking

We tend to see ourselves in black and white with very little gray area. We are either good or bad. This is dangerous because we see only success or failure not progression. It's not worth it if I can't __ (win, get promoted, be the star, etc.). You fill in the blank. There are a lot of opportunities available in the nuances between the cracks—we can't afford to be binary or we'll miss the many opportunities for joy, new possibilities and growth.

• Over-generalization

You see a single event as a never-ending buffet of disappointment. "This always happens to me; I can't get a break." Infinitives like, "always, never, ever, all the time," are typically not accurate or true. They are dangerous thoughts because they paint on such a large canvas. They present a self-imposed roadblock that we can't get around. Catch yourself and others using these words-they're easy red flags to spot.

• Jumping to Conclusions

Speculating to the negative with no real information, in record time. A new personal best! We often do this in the absence of a benefit of the doubt.

• Emotional Reasoning

We convince ourselves that our emotional state is an accurate representation of what is happening around us. We tell ourselves, "I feel something so it must be real."

• Magnification

Blowing things up and out of proportion. Making mountains

out of mole hills. I have never seen a mole hill, but I'm assuming they are smaller than a mountain. Exaggerating to the negative.

These are just a few examples of the dangerous cognitive traps we can fall into. But here is the punch line. What will happen if we put less negative input into the system? What will happen if we dismantle *Cognitive Distortion* as it starts to form? The same thing that happens every time we take an informed, purposeful step forward—things improve and we grow.

EMOTIONAL HEALTH: Self-Esteem

Our sense of "self" is incredibly complicated. It begins very early in life and can be influenced positively and negatively by a myriad of events along the way. It rises when we win and plummets when we fail. We unwittingly place our sense of self into the hands of others expecting them to curate it on our behalf. Much of how we see ourselves today is part of a fabric woven with inputs we have received from experiences and individuals throughout our lives, Indeed, a whole bushel of insecurities have been cast upon us. What now?

We usually laugh when we think about toothy self-help advocates sharing their enthusiasm for the power of self-love. Perhaps we should stop and listen. We know the score; we even have an idea of what created our self-esteem issues (which is historically really interesting but has no value short of where to focus our forgiveness). So, what can we do, at least partially, to take ownership and control? We may always be open to the sting of criticism and failure, but if we can positively and purposefully energize and rebuild our self-esteem, we can recover faster.

• Self-Affirmations

This one will probably take some selling. All I can picture in my mind is the *Saturday Night Live* Stuart Smalley skit, "I'm good enough, I'm smart enough, and gosh darn it, people like me. I am a worthy human, darn you mom." We know they make for great TV comedy but are they real? Do self-affirmations actually work? As a matter of fact, they are unbelievably powerful and many of the most successful individuals in the world embrace their positive influence[12]. Wait, what? Really? Yep.

I don't think you should get into the habit of affirmations just because Oprah, Jim Carey, Denzel Washington and Jennifer Lopez do. But I do think it's well worth your effort to make it part of your purposeful emotional health strategy. Here's how and why it works.

Self-affirmations and acknowledgements are simply word statements we say to ourselves or out loud. We occupy our thoughts considering our awesomeness. Do you need to believe everything you tell yourself? No. But you do need to repeat positive affirmations over and over. Eventually they'll seep into your sub-conscience. Our sub-conscience mind can't tell the difference between a wonderful dream and reality. I have friends like that.

We already know that our thoughts are occupied with the input we provide; positive, neutral or negative. When we affirm and acknowledge our strengths and accomplishments, we color our mood with positive tones. We replace the negative speculation with purposeful mantras that fuel our emotional health and help us achieve our goals.

• Affirmations Exercise

Make a list of your strengths. Now start adding anything and everything positive about you. In a best-case scenario, these are traits, capabilities and attitudes that you may need to accomplish something specific in your life strategy.

I am; loyal, a great friend, creative, tireless, capable, always learning, focused on what's important, a dedicated partner, a hard worker. I am; intelligent, a great brother or sister, my personality wins, I'm a great listener, I am perfect in my design... keep going!

Formalize this list of affirmations by writing them down and read them to yourself aloud every morning. Color your world before you ever leave the house. Take control, regulate your emotions through affirmations. Fill your mind with purposeful positive truths about yourself. I'm not advocating self-delusion here, "truths" is the vital operative word. Focus on them and there won't be any room for negative, self-destructive mind-scripts.

• Disengage from Negative Input

News, conversations, friends, the water cooler, social media —get out of any hate and criticism cycles. Turn the faucet off, let the sink drain. It's true we are what we eat. If our appetite includes hate, depravity, sensationalism and drama, that's what we will put on the table. If we pursue positive, enriching input, even if it's self-produced, we will set a table of opportunity. We will expand the field of opportunity at play in our life.

I do my affirmations at the end of my meditation. Yes meditation. It's amazing, powerful and it integrates easily into a life wellness plan. There's a very low entry barrier here, try it! Ten or fifteen minutes, once or twice a day. I would recommend an online learning course—Lisa and I took one online by Emily Fletcher called, *Ziva Meditation*—I recommend it. Pick one that appeals to you. This can be especially effective in reducing stress and anxiety.

I don't want to try to teach meditation; I'm not qualified, but I can personally endorse its powerful impact in my life. It was captivating from the first time I tried it and continues to create value in my life. Even the shallowest, clumsiest efforts stabilize and give me control over my emotional well-being.

The initial phase, "mindfulness", is a simple process. Breathe purposefully—in for two, out for four, in for three, out for six. Repeat and feel your stomach distend as you inhale deeply, exhaling (metaphorically) from the base of your spine.

Next, run through each of your senses. Focus on your skin, from your toes to your head, the feel of clothing, warmth, coolness. Then listen. What do you hear? What do you smell? Breathe deeply to focus on the aroma. What can you see through your mind's eye? What is in the room? What's the taste inside your mouth? Then feel it all together.

I am oversimplifying something that deserves study and understanding. I want to remove the mystery about meditation. I had all kinds of distorted ideas about what it was, how you do it and why. What I learned immediately was the act of mindfulness was incredibly powerful. It takes you out of the screenplay we are imagining and brings us right smack dab in the middle of what is actually happening in our life right at this moment. That, my friends, is incredibly powerful. We live on the horizon, speculating and wasting a staggering amount of time and energy, jousting with emotional windmills.

Toward the end of my fifteen-minute meditation, I insert my affirmations and acknowledgments. I create the input I will use to add form, dimension and color to my day. "I am a vessel of grace, I have great patience, my smile dismantles fear, I speak evenly without overt emotion." Then, when someone comes up to me at the coffee bar and asks, "How's it going?" and I say "Awesome", they look at me with great disappointment, "Oh, okay well that must be nice." "It is!" I tell them, "And it's a choice, choose awesome."

I started responding this way when I realized most people were asking me how I was doing so they could reciprocate with how absolutely shitty their weekend was. It pretty much stopped those negativity dumps that people want to take. Try it. Take control of your emotional health. Be aware of the pitfalls of cognitive distortions. Make a list of affirmations and purposefully reprogram your sub-conscience mind.

III. SPIRITUAL HEALTH

This can be an elusive topic for many of us. The term "spirituality" has been redefined over time. Many people associate the term with formalized religion. That makes sense given its early usage referred to a process of reformatting ourselves to the intended, original design of man. Christianity, for example, identifies with the Holy Spirit in this context.

Today, the scope of the meaning of spirituality is broad and individualistic. No matter what spiritual belief you recognize, they all share something in common: they take us out of the earthly, material world and force us to consider things much bigger than ourselves. It's a facet of who we are and if we ignore it, we will feel the void. We are the only life form on earth that can channel the unique and powerful potential of spirituality. It's there for a reason.

Spirituality is connectivity. It aligns us to something greater than ourselves. We gain a sense of belonging and purpose. Our values and beliefs are shaped by our spirituality. Our sense of right and wrong, good and bad. We take on a perspective that things happen for a reason which releases us from the whirlpool of, "Why?" Our lives are more than just a roll of the dice.

Our spirituality helps us process difficult matters of the heart, loss and failure. It guides our personal journey, shapes our view of the world and our role in it. In a violent and sensationalistic world, it suggests grace, peace, harmony and forgiveness. Our spirituality is the well-spring of knowledge and wisdom we derive from within ourselves.

When we are leveraging *Spiritual Health*, we find beauty in things, our respect for our environment increases and it drives us to a higher standard. It reconnects us to each other and our world in a positive and caring way. Spirituality makes us nicer than we are without it. We need it. Without it, we run the risk of falling into an existential hole, left wondering who we are and why we are.

If this is a void in your life, your life is out of balance. The lack of spirituality can manifest itself in so many destructive ways. We can experience a lack of self-esteem, a negative outlook, anger, moral decline, we can't let things go, we hold grudges, we experience anxiety and a host of other issues. It all manifests when we are suffering from a lack of spirituality in our lives. *Spiritual Health* is a powerful, positive differentiator that gives Gig Rockers an elevated human edge to their interpersonal relationships.

When it comes to making a spiritual connection, we have many options available. Christianity, Islam, Hinduism, Buddhism, African Traditional, Judaism, Sikhism, Spiritism, Bahai and Shinto are just a few of the possibilities in the ocean of spiritual belief systems. Maybe one is right for you. There are 4,300 religious groups active on a global level. Mankind has a burning, spiritual thirst for "a reason." We know, just like water, spiritual awareness is essential to our survival. If you're an atheist, perhaps try Humanism—find equilibrium, a moral compass, care for your fellow humans.

Spiritual Health doesn't necessarily mean formalized religion, church and community. There are other ways to ignite and elevate your *Spiritual Health*.

• Knowledge

Study spiritual topics to learn about a belief system or learn about several. Become a student of spiritual things, thoughts and behaviors. Determine what resonates with you and why. Uncover the history of man's spiritual journey. Today's media options make it so easy. Netflix and YouTube, to name two, have a whole host of documentary style films available. Study, think and grow your Spiritual IQ.

• Meditation

Nope, I'm not letting this go, it's too good. The practice of meditation can be applied to spiritual thoughts. An unencumbered self can more easily explore the possibilities of spirituality. We start to see the order and design of things and where we fit. The sum of this flows into our emotional health and on to our physical health in a continuous cycle of renewal within our personal ecosystem.

• Serving

There is something about serving that activates and fuels our spiritual need. As a cancer survivor, I am compelled to encourage and inspire others that face this challenge. I'm not sure who benefits more, me or the people I'm trying to help. When I focus on and invest in serving others, I feel good about my spiritual self, I feel good about me.

• Journey

In Australian Aboriginal culture, young men go on a solo wilderness experience for up to six months. "The Walkabout" is a rite of manhood, but it is also a spiritual journey, a time of spiritual awakening. Yeshua walked in the desert for 40 days fasting, praying and battling demons to prepare himself. There is value in disconnecting. There is value in disconnecting. It's not a typo, I said it twice. We tend to feel guilty if we unplug for even a moment, let alone 40 days.

I'm not saying you need to go to Coachella, trip your way to spiritual enlightenment and write some cool songs along the way, I am saying, disconnect, unplug, or in the words of Frank Zappa, "Dis-cor-por-ate, and come with me"[13]. Jump the matrix, escape and turn your thoughts away from earthly matters.

An easy way to actualize this concept of "journey" on a more attainable scale and integrate Spiritual Health into our daily routine is to simply take a walk. Take a walk by ourselves and think about things, listen to our hearts, feel the connection to nature and enjoy the sense of belonging. Your spiritual instincts will speak to you if you quell the background noise. Take a walk and consider spiritual things.

If your goal is to elevate, to lean-in and Rock Your Gig, you must persue balance within your personal ecosystem.

- **Spiritual Summation**

Don't put your life out of balance by neglecting your spirituality. It's too important, and so easy to fix. Don't allow yourself to rationalize that you are fine without it, you're not. Don't confuse spirituality with religion, they are not mutually exclusive. Both are available a la carte and as a combo meal. If it isn't elevating you, it's not *Spiritual Health*. Guilt is not *Spiritual Health*. The sound of your coins dropping in a plate is not *Spiritual Health*. Coming into church late and sitting in the first row so everyone knows you're there is not *Spiritual Health*.

Joy, grace, humility, understanding, acceptance, compassion, serving, caring, loving, listening, persevering, inspiring, learning, and forgiving are some of the hallmarks of strong *Spiritual Health*. Think about infusing these traits into your relationships, your work, your children. Understand their impact on your emotions and health. Pursuing spiritual balance will enhance every facet of your life. Go get ya some!

INTEGRATED BALANCE

To review, we have identified three domains of personal focus; *Physical Health, Emotional Health* and *Spiritual Health*.

We understand that our investment and focus in these areas create a fertile environment for growth. They support and serve the health of the ecosystem of "you." All three elements are interconnected and influence one another. A breakdown in our physical wellbeing can adversely affect our emotional health, while improvements in our physical health fuel positive emotions and self-esteem.

The *Rock Your Gig* perspective takes "balance" out of the traditional pie-wheel and throws it onto Mr. Spock's three-dimensional chessboard. You didn't see that episode? Sorry, more Star Trek, I digress. We don't want a flat perspective of work, relationships, spirituality, friendship, romance, finances etc. These are all very important elements of our lives, but we tend to segment them from one another as stand-alone entities. We ignore the interconnected, multi-dimensional nature of the ecosystem. We systematically assemble the rationalizations and write Pulitzer Prize winning excuses to justify indefinitely putting off a balanced approach to our lives. But like Mr. Spock's multi-tiered chess board, balance requires us to move the pieces up, down, over and back, to create a winning life strategy. Ok, I'm not a "Trekkie", but if you're unfamiliar, treat yourself to some old school *Star Trek* sometime, there's wisdom to be had.

Our lives are busy and complicated. We tell ourselves, "My life is too busy and too complicated." We surrender in defeat before the battle begins. We need a new perspective. A problem-solving perspective. We need to dismantle our limiting belief systems and build new empowering monuments that encourage and enable.

In *Rock Your Gig* fashion, we'll start with an *Objective Self-Assessment*. It's an exercise that takes a harder look at our lives and the distribution of enhancing experiences. We'll use the *Life Balance Assessment Tool* template in this chapter to give form to your thinking. Be honest, we are looking for opportunities. Use the 1 to 5 scale to represent qualitative or quantitative high points. This isn't an assessment to determine if you have life balance, the purpose is to identify areas we may be neglecting, seize them as opportunities and start engineering a plan to improvee your life balance.

LIFE BALANCE ASSESSMENT

	1	2	3	4	5
Physical	◯	◯	◯	◯	◯
Financial	◯	◯	◯	◯	◯
Friendships	◯	◯	◯	◯	◯
Me	◯	◯	◯	◯	◯
Spiritual	◯	◯	◯	◯	◯
Work	◯	◯	◯	◯	◯
Rest	◯	◯	◯	◯	◯
Learning	◯	◯	◯	◯	◯
Fun	◯	◯	◯	◯	◯
Family	◯	◯	◯	◯	◯
Romance	◯	◯	◯	◯	◯
Serving	◯	◯	◯	◯	◯
Community	◯	◯	◯	◯	◯
Nature	◯	◯	◯	◯	◯
Creativity	◯	◯	◯	◯	◯
TV	◯	◯	◯	◯	◯

NOTE: I suggest you copy _Life Balance Assessment_ page and keep the original clean. You may want to share this exercise with others or even re-take the assessment say, a year from now, and examine your progress.

EVALUATION & INTEGRATION

Our belief system is this: If we can find a way to touch each of these elements, or a great percentage of them, consistently and with quality, we will optimize our personal ecosystem. And when that happens, everything just seems to flow with less restriction.

So how did you do? Oh, you haven't done it yet. I bet you glanced at it. Either way, this is the first step. Where are we ringing the bell and where is it dead quiet? The first time I did this I nailed it. Of the sixteen triggers, I was effective and engaged in three. My optimistic son Micah would say, "That's pretty good, you got three." If I was being honest with myself, I would have realized I was neglecting, ignoring, running like hell from 80% of the power-inducing opportunities in life.

We want to look for the opportunities to integrate some of these elements into the dominant verticals in our life, like work and home. On a continuum, our employment can span a wide range of structure and responsibility. There are factory assembly roles that require focus and repetitive processes, and there are freestyle sales roles. Whatever our employment scenario, possibilities exist to integrate life balance.

For example: Get up from your desk and take a walk on your next break. Don't go to the vending machine, go for a walk. While you're on that ten minute walk, call your mom, play a song, think spiritual thoughts, take a photo, send it to a friend, put your feet in the grass, stop and sit on a bench, turn your closed eyes toward the sun. When you have had your fill of vitamin D, sashay back to the office, the factory, the hospital, the 23rd floor or the house and get back to business. This simple example hits eight of the sixteen sweet spots of Balance.

Sit in a quiet room, in your car or under a tree and meditate for ten minutes. Affirm your positive potential while you uncouple from the machine. Take your family on a bike ride to watch the sunset. Oh, you get home too late? How about a sunrise? Full moon? Solar eclipse? Get off the couch, put down your device and play a board game with your kids, go to your mom's house and rake her leaves. Oh, you do that already? You're a good person. Take a night class with your partner! Start a community outreach program with your kids. We've just identified eight opportunities to elevate and energize our ecosystem.

THE TIME MYTH

The best all-purpose excuse is without a doubt, "I don't have time." Oh, you didn't say that, did you? Let's break it down like James Brown, bring the band down behind me boys, I need to testify, don't shout me down while I tell the simple truth about time.

• **Work:** "I work 50 hours a week." That's a few more than the average American who comes in at 47 hours week. We are all working harder these days.

50 hours

• **Commute:** "I commute about a half-hour, depending on traffic." That's consistent with the national average, according to the US Census Bureau statistic of 25.4 minutes.[14]

5 hours

• **Sleep:** "I have to get 8 hours or I'm a beast." Must be nice.

56 hours

• **Physical:** "I work out for an hour five days a week." Seriously? Five hours a week? Your fellow Americans, all 23% of the populations that exercise, do an average of 150 minutes a week, about 20 minutes a day. Generous.

4 hours

• **Family:** "I spend two hours a night with my kids, my girlfriend, my dog..." Lots of variables here. Are you single? Married with kids? Let's say you work a full shift and spend a focused two hours a day on family (being in your family's presence, in the same room on your phone, isn't engagement by the way).

14 hours

• **Personal:** "I shower, shave, do my hair, and do some laundry and the dishes." Ok Cinderella, I believe you.

6 hours

TOTAL:

135 hours

"Yeah, but you left out a lot of stuff, I go to the grocery store, and get the car washed, and mow the lawn, and I take my kids to soccer practice..." Ok, Ok, I see that you are a very busy individual, I get it. I know you never sit mindlessly in front of the television watching sensationalistic negative trash. I know you don't spend hours on Facebook peeping into the lives of people you don't know. I know that your time is a toddler in a tierra... short and precious. I get it. Let's give you another 8-hours credit, the equivalent of an extra workday.

TOTAL:

143 hours

That's a pretty generous distribution of time. Most of us don't have all these dynamics in play. Some of us do, and the need for thoughtful integration is even more critical. In this pretty aggressive scenario, we've come up with 143 applied hours.

TOTAL AVAILABLE HOURS IN EVERY WEEK:

168 hours

In this "very full life" model, there are still 25 hours open. That's a part time job if you need to eliminate debt, time enough to start a business, workout ...hell you could open a gym with that much time, go to night school, day school, dog grooming school, get a Real Estate license. Stop making time your excuse. Stop telling yourself you're too busy to enhance your freaking life. It's simply not true.

While I'm on a roll, lets address time in the larger sense. "I'm too old to ___." fill in the blank. I understand this one. I was a product of the 1960s "Flower Power" generation. I thought life ended right around 47—you know, when you got old. At 61, with the libido of a raging monk, energy and hair, I know that was a misconception. The *Spirit of Reinvention* is alive in me, my passion to learn and grow is just as intense as it ever was. I see nothing but potential on the horizon, and you should too. Don't let your age lie to you about what time it is.

REWIND: BALANCE in the ECOSYSTEM of YOU

Balance:

Balance in the ecosystem creates positive energy and drives elevated interpersonal relationships. It increases the output and potential of positive connectivity.

When the ecosystem is in balance it brings energy, clarity and focus to our interactions. When it is out of balance our interpersonal effectiveness is compromised.

Physical Health, Emotional Health and Spiritual Health:

Rock Your Gig focuses on and takes an integrated holistic view of these three internal factors that influence the health of the *Personal Ecosystem*.

I. Physical Health: (page 42)

Don't ignore the signs of compromised physical health, don't wait until something breaks. Start small, educate yourself about food, exercise, rest.

Cognitive Distortion: (page 46)

Emotional wellbeing isn't being "happy" all the time, it's about self-awareness and self-regulation. It's about controlling emotions, not eliminating or denying them. Cognitive distortions can derail your interpersonal effectiveness.

II. Emotional Health: (page 48)

Within the context of *Rock Your Gig*, Emotional health is about being in a state of awareness with the ability to control and regulate our emotions, feelings, thoughts and behaviors.

III. Spiritual Health: (page 51)

It may come in many packages. Don't confuse *Spiritual Health* and religion. They are not mutually exclusive. Elevate your spiritual awareness through Knowledge, Meditation, Serving and Journey.

Integrated Balance: (page 54)

Integrated Balance is the distribution of enhancing experiences. The *Rock Your Gig* philosophy takes them from a vertical orientation to look for integration opportunities. Physical with work, spiritual with physical.

The Time Myth: (page 58)

"I don't have the time." is a lousy excuse. Get a real accounting of how you spend your time. Don't let your age lie to about what time it is. Go for it.

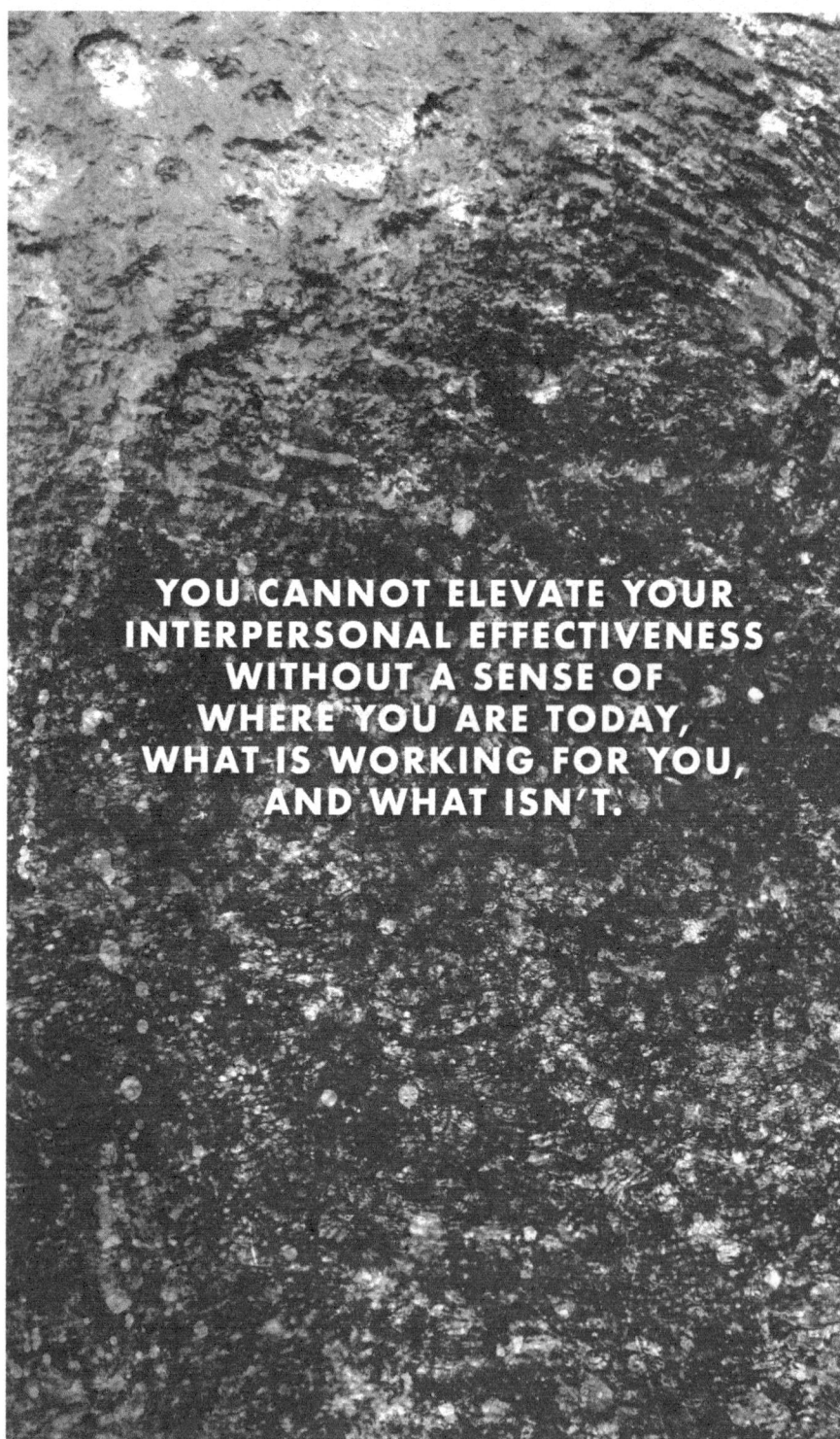

YOU CANNOT ELEVATE YOUR
INTERPERSONAL EFFECTIVENESS
WITHOUT A SENSE OF
WHERE YOU ARE TODAY,
WHAT IS WORKING FOR YOU,
AND WHAT ISN'T.

CHAPTER 4

OBJECTIVE SELF-ASSESSMENT

CHAPTER 4.

OBJECTIVE SELF-ASSESSMENT

I want to stay calibrated. The macro objective of *Rock Your Gig* is to elevate your interpersonal awareness and effectiveness to drive inspired, productive and sustainable relationships. We want relationships that rock and an audience roaring for an encore. To accomplish this, we need to embrace the spirit of reinvention and improve our interpersonal effectiveness: ultimately to become individuals who extend themselves to create strong connections with others.

When it's time to take it to the bridge and break it down like James Brown, our first riff has to be *Objective Self-Assessment*. This process can help identify areas of opportunity or the need for reinvention. You cannot elevate your interpersonal effectiveness without a sense of where you are today, what is working for you, and what isn't.

It doesn't matter where you fall on the need for reinvention continuum, the best place to start is *Objective Self-Assessment*. We can apply a business forensics mechanic known as the "post-mortem" to our professional or personal circumstances. This is simply an in-depth look at the results and the validity of the belief system that established the expectations. In other words,

***What* did we *believe* would happened?**

***Why* did we *think* it would happen?**

***What actually* happened?**

Remember, reinvention is also situational—there may be one primary area of focus for you or your business. Perhaps it's an issue that has been affecting you for some time and you haven't been able to drive sustainable change. These are potential candidate areas for reinvention and should reveal themselves through self-assessment.

An example from my life was weight loss. I was always an XL guy, six foot and 195 pounds, all through my 30s. By the time I was forty-five I was still six feet tall, but I weighed 300 pounds! I carried it well. People were shocked if I told them what I weighed. I stopped looking at the scale at 296 pounds, a cinnamon Pop-Tart from 300, and kept on eating

My self-esteem was taking a hit; I hated myself in photos and videos which I had to do frequently as part of my role as Fender's front man. I remember being on ABC news in New York City doing a piece with evening news anchor David Muir. He was late, as many media types often are. It was summer in the city, hot and humid. I was so uncomfortable, so overweight that I sweat when I ate. I had to change my shirt before the broadcast. The pain of being overweight was finally eclipsing the pleasure of eating like a Viking. But I still didn't lose weight.

Fast forward four years, I have survived stage-three cancer, brain surgery to remove the cancerous tumor, radiation treatments, sixteen months of chemotherapy and naturopathic infusion remedies. If you saw me, you would never know I had been so ill. I took cancer on nose-to-nose and won. And I still weighed three-hundred-freaking-pounds!

I had lost weight during chemo, but it all came back once I started to recover from the treatments. Over the years I had tried the various fad diets. Low carb diets worked for a bit. All were temporary solutions at best. You start rationalizing and lying to yourself; its genetic, I have a condition, everyone in my family is heavy, the sun's in my eyes, I tripped on a rock… Eventually we take it off the table as an unsolvable problem.

Good morning Mr. McDonald, this is your wake-up call.

My beautiful daughter Charlee, who was seven at the time, met me at the door one evening after work. When I say met me at the door, I mean she met me at the door. The moment I opened it she extended her hand to me and walked us toward the kitchen. She informed me, "Mommy has something to tell you." We walked together into the kitchen where she presented me to my wife, Lisa. "Mommy, go ahead." I had no idea what was about to come at me.

Over the next few minutes, Lisa reviewed the results of a physical I had taken a couple of weeks prior. The results were disappointing. Actually, they were frightening. I had just dusted myself off after several rounds in the ring with my glioma friend and now this? Critically high blood pressure (which I admit I should have known), cholesterol through the roof, and ready to be the next customer being served in the type 2 diabetes line. This was one of those, piano-falls-on-your-head-from-the-third-story wakeup calls that screamed reinvention. It was time to take a serious look in the mirror and try to see the truth. It was the opening set, and the first two songs were *Post-mortem* and *Objective Self Assessment*. Oddly enough, weight loss was the wrong goal. The need to lose weight was only an answer to a symptom of something I should have been paying more attention to, a symptom of something even bigger. I wouldn't have figured that out if I hadn't stopped and done a robust post mortem on my life's health patterns, beliefs, behaviors and outcomes. I questioned everything that was status quo that had impacted my health, directly or indirectly. What I discovered amazed me.

That family intervention laid the foundation for what would become my new and improved approach to health. None of this would have happened without thoughtful self-assessment and the spirit of reinvention. The result was weight loss (over 100 pounds), but the positive impact of this reinvention on my life was broader and more significant than just the weight loss. All three medical conditions—blood pressure, cholesterol and pre-diabetics were reversed in one year without the use of medication. Sixteen months of chemo will cure you of the love of medications as a remedy for anything. My knees, ankles, feet, hips, shoulders, neck and back all realized significant pain relief. I felt better, slept better, was more alert, more active, more energized, more fun to be around, more effective and as hard as it is to believe… better looking, as a result of this introspective evaluation and reinvention.

Oddly enough, weight loss was the wrong goal. The need to lose weight was only an answer to a symptom of something I should have been paying more attention to, a symptom of something even bigger. I wouldn't have figured that out if I hadn't stopped and done a robust post-mortem on my life's health patterns, beliefs, behaviors and outcomes. I questioned everything that was a status quo that had impacted my health, directly or indirectly. What I discovered during my post-mortem amazed me.

I had very few real, educated, unbiased points of view about food other than whether I liked it, or had eaten it recently. My belief system was antiquated and ill-informed. I didn't really know how much I ate from a caloric perspective, where my food came from, what nutrients they contain, where protein actually comes from, (versus what I believed and had been sold—oops, I mean told). Ultimately, my health reinvention required a committed journey of learning and experimentation. I had to gain the perspectives needed to build a new belief system. A belief system that contributed to my health. Elements of the reinvention were immediate choices (like my choice to be vegan), while others were more linear behavioral changes that evolved as I tuned-in to the signals my body had desperately been trying to send. Reinvention creates a new state of being, it's not temporal, it's not a shortcut, it's a new path.

Empowered by the *Spirit of Reinvention* and leveraging the processes of *Self-Assessment* and *Strategic Planning* I built a bridge to better health, and lost one hundred pounds along the way. You can too. Let's take a look at our second *Objective Assessment* tool. **The Personal S.W.O.T.**

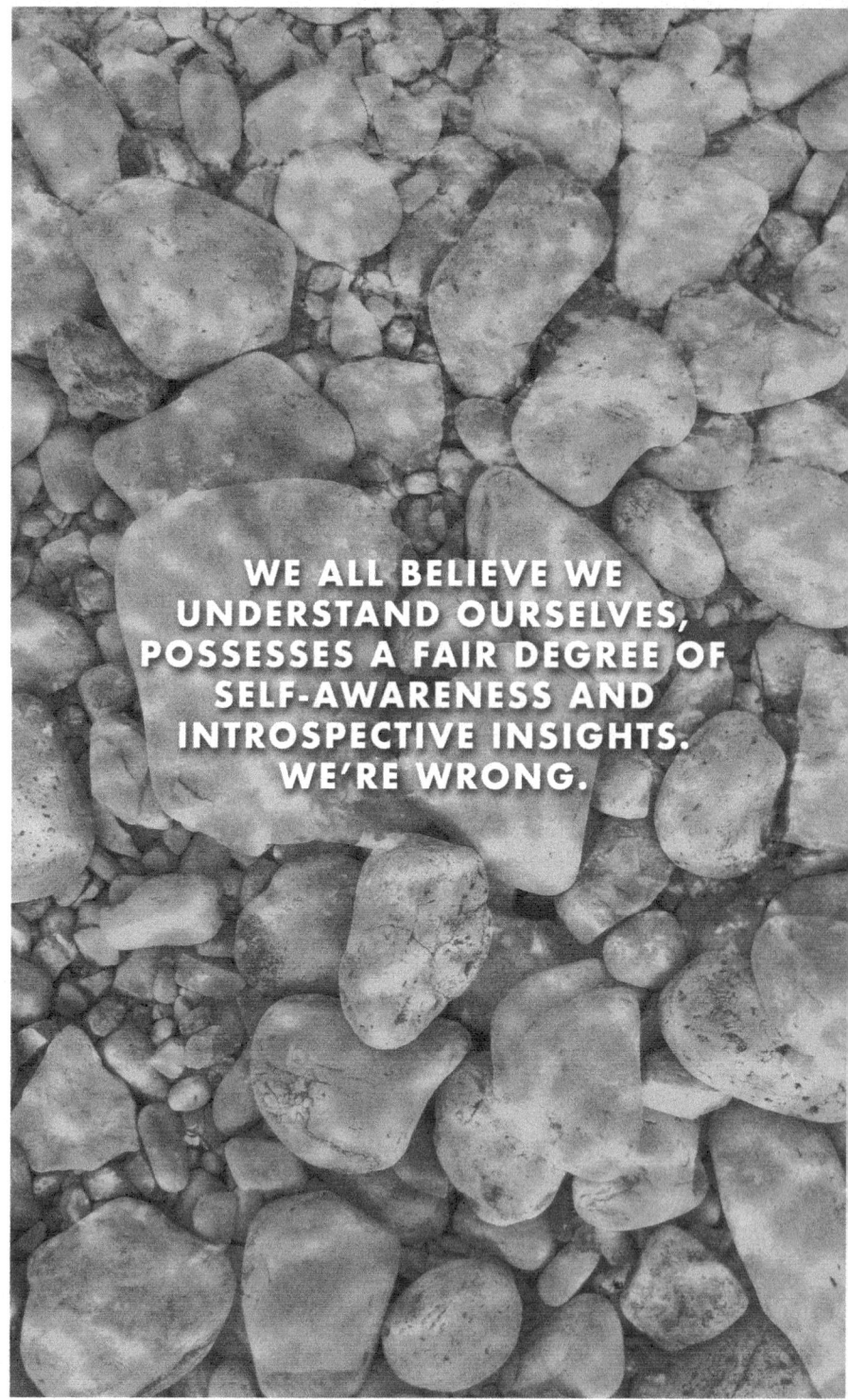

WE ALL BELIEVE WE
UNDERSTAND OURSELVES,
POSSESSES A FAIR DEGREE OF
SELF-AWARENESS AND
INTROSPECTIVE INSIGHTS.
WE'RE WRONG.

CHAPTER 5

S.W.O.T. ANALYSIS

CHAPTER 5.
S.W.O.T ANALYSIS

The odds are high you are familiar with the term SWOT analysis. The acronym stands for *Strengths, Weaknesses, Opportunities* and *Threats*. The tool was created by Albert Humphrey while working at the Stanford Research Institute in London. SWOT is a strategic planning method used in evaluating specific projects or the feasibility of business opportunities. It was adopted, and has been widely used, as an evaluation tool for the purposes of career growth.

INTERNAL   EXTERNAL

5a. Traditional internal / external SWOT model

The traditional model is organized with *Strengths* and *Weaknesses* as *Internal* factors, *Opportunities* and *Threats* as *External* factors. Classic examples of *External* factors include; competitive threats, capabilities, individuals competing for roles or business you want, changes in regulatory landscape and countless others.

Internalized SWOT

For our purpose, which is *Objective Self-Assessment*, we are going to modify the traditional SWOT. The first change is simple, we shift our perspectives regarding opportunities and threats from an *external* survey, to an *internal* survey. In this way, we transform the SWOT to focus on our human potential. The tool helps us stay objective when looking inward, which is not the easiest thing to do. When it comes to evaluating "Us", we have some serious biases to deal with. The process and tool will keep us focused on the real, definable and actionable issues.

5b. *Rock Your Gig* internal SWOT model

Before we begin, a few notes. This is a skill that has to be developed. It doesn't come naturally for most of us. Honest, objective self-assessment is hard. It's a core theme of *Rock Your Gig*, and it doesn't end here. The focus shouldn't be on creating an architectural masterpiece depicting your life strategy. The goal is to start a new habit—to take on a new way of looking at your life and create a more purposeful, aware, focused path to fulfillment.

First Steps

The first time you sit down to do this may be a bit clumsy and feel like a waste of time. Depending on your *Personality Design* (we'll get to *Personality Designs* in Chapters 6 and 7), you may be ready to move along already. If so, slow down, take a breath, it's just the first set. *Rock Your Gig's* mission is to ignite a spark of *Objective Self-Assessment* and offer you a format and tools you can use to get started. If in the end, you adopt these practices, this will become a regular part of your ongoing, personal evolution and you will get a lot better at it. It's also important to understand that it is situational–your strengths and weaknesses play out differently depending on the context. Team is a huge element to consider. You don't have to be all things, to all people (to be on a team, that is).

Seek Input

Another tip I hope you will consider, is to recruit the feedback of others that know you well. Individuals that can be at least somewhat transparent and honest with you, have a unique perspective and can be an advocate if you are shortchanging yourself. On the other hand, you may not feel comfortable exposing your personal growth interest or just prefer to keep it "in house." That is more often the case than not. These are personal journeys. But as you review the material ahead, people you trust that can comfortably provide valuable perspectives will come to mind—don't be afraid to engage them. We often err in the accounting of our strengths. A thoughtful acquaintance may be able to point something out you are missing. It's also a great exercise for couples. No shortage of honest, direct feedback from that source.

S.: STRENGTHS

APPLIED STRENGTHS

The purpose of the SWOT is to evaluate all the stuff we do well, our "cosmic muscle" so-to-speak. It is the amalgamation of the skills and talents we possess, the proficiencies and knowledge we have developed along life's journey. The entire compliment of our positive capabilities, refined over time by experience, wins and losses, and everything we naturally possess as a benefit of our perfect design, are traits we use to relate and connect with others. We also use these traits to generate income through employment and achieve our life's ambitions. Focusing and leveraging strengths can be highly productive. But first, we need to look at our strengths in a new light, then we can begin to analyze how we can leverage them in meaningful, relevant ways.

Some of our strengths are all-purpose and serve us in many unique and varied situations. We probably take some of them for granted, it's just "who we are." Communication skills, integrity, attention to detail, grace and honor—we establish these strengths through education, experience, hobbies and passions. Most of us also possess what we refer to as, "Inherited

Strengths", i.e. "My creativity comes from my mother's side of the family."

ACTUALIZED STRENGTHS

The principal of *Applied Strengths* examines each independent strength trait through specific situational lenses. Our strengths are not actualized until we apply them to the right circumstance, at the right time, in the right way. To help organize our thoughts, we will need to distill the applications to those opportunities that create tangible results.

For the purposes of career progression, let's focus on four key areas. These are the cornerstones of our Strengths Assessment:

1. Getting Things Done

This strength trait helps us achieve results. Focus, energy and adaptability all serve us when we are driving for the finish line. These strengths can be observed in home projects, work challenges, hobbies, philanthropy–wherever there is a clear, definable finish line.

2. Strategic Energy

This strength trait is often evidenced in the areas of planning, vision, creative or in analytics. Do you have a competitive nature that helps you see opportunity? Do you enjoy research and defining solutions? Are you comfortable with risk? If so, that's a strength that will serve you well as a strategic thinker.

3. Bridge Building

This strength trait is embodied in versatility... and it's a good one, I might add. Do you step outside your comfort zone to relate to others? Are you collaborative and an effective communicator? Is your self-awareness a strength? ... or maybe a weakness?

4. Influencing Others

The signs of this strength trait are seen in articulate, passionate and inspiring communicators. Are you in Sales or Marketing? Are you a great listener? How's your charisma? Come on, don't be shy. Are you comfortable on stage, self-confident and committed? Mothers and schoolteachers leverage influence strengths all day long.

We can use these category lenses to collect, focus and organize our data. This is not a mental exercise! Take the assessment, acknowledge the results and formalize action. It needs to be written down, carved in stone, tattooing may be extreme, but short of that, write it down. Keep it visible. Make it real!

If you and I were sitting together and I asked you to share your personal strengths, I imagine many of you would not have a real problem answering the question. We all possess some sense of self in this regard. So, let's start with stuff we are good at and then explore the areas where we may lack confidence.

WHERE to LOOK for APPLIED STRENGTHS

Everywhere! "Always be on the lookout" works as a philosophy, but it doesn't really help us get started. We know our strengths are only measurable when we are leveraging them. Where do we leverage the characteristic strengths associated with 1. Getting Things Done. 2. Strategic Energy. 3. Bridge Building and 4. Influencing Others?

To search for examples let's look at a four category formula of applied strengths; Early Life Equity + Educational Journey + Employment History + Home.

• Early Life Equity

Early life equity is quite often the most overlooked area of a *Personal Strengths Assessment*. Typically, I would have to pull it out of young professionals in career growth sessions. You don't see it on resumes and when you ask a candidate to walk you through their bio, they don't offer many clues. In my case, it was music and specifically guitar. I spent an inordinate amount of time playing guitar, thinking about playing guitar, dreaming about guitars—and I still do today. If you had told me that someday I would be "The Guy" designing Fender guitars and amps, I would have laughed at you in disbelief. Twenty-five years later, I was hiring people just like me—guitar crazy kids that stayed with their passion and made it a profession. If you have just graduated from high school or finished a university degree, been forced to find a new career path, or if you are just bored with what you are doing, this exercise can be incredibly helpful and revealing.

Keep in mind, we aren't building a resume, we are performing an internally focused objective self-assessment. We are collecting and contemplating our personal strengths. Don't overlook the experiences of your youth:

Just because you were young doesn't nullify their value. Those experiences may be the key to finding your passion and true fulfillment. It's always easier to rock a gig you love.

If you played a sport consistently and loved it, participated in band, yearbook or quill and scroll society, built cars with your dad, rode dirt bikes or horses, played on the golf team, played guitar, became an Eagle Scout, volunteered at your church, traveled extensively–these are all extremely valuable personal strength guideposts. Was there a consistent, driving passion you were engaged in from age 8 to 20 years? Is there a pattern to your varied interest over time?

When contemplating the *Intangibles for Life Equity*, don't forget the adjacent, connected activities and all of the satellites orbiting your interest. Where there any you really enjoyed? I have a lot of musician friends that are crazy about the gear. They love all the equipment that comes with playing, recording and performing, whether they record and perform or not. They're just as interested in talking about the equipment as they are playing. Others have no clue, no interest and no time for guitar gear, they have what works for them and they just want to play.

We are looking for your passion: the things you did because you *wanted* to, not because you *had* to. If you had passion for something and went deep into it, it has value. You absolutely leveraged a personal strength as you pursued your life's passions.

• Educational Journey

This is a great box to unpack. It can reveal a lot about our strengths and weaknesses, if we look through the right lenses. The formal educational process is a long one. In some people's cases, really long. It's also challenging, frustrating, stressful, inspiring, empowering, demotivating, fun, miserable, awesome, expensive—and so much more.

We don't typically stop to think about it in its entirety. When was it fun and why? When was it miserable and why? When did you feel the most energized? The answers to these questions are vitally important. They reveal where our strengths and passions came alive and served us well. This line of questioning also reminds us of the areas where we struggled, that created anxiety.

If you are an engineer by trade or a financial analyst, the odds are high that you were always a little better at math than the other kids. Your work was a little more precise perhaps? *Of course* it was! Analytical energy is a strength you possess. You may also be an incredibly gifted artist, but it doesn't negate your strength in analytical areas like mathematics. Use the intellectual and emotional triggers of your educational journey to bring your strengths and weaknesses to light.

• Employment History

This activity represents the apex of our engagement, effort and energy on a daily basis. We are at our most visible, most connected state-of-being when employed. We use our minds, our backs, our book smarts and street cred. We buy and sell, barter, build, plan, create and debate. The scope and intensity are no different for the stay-at-home parent than for the Fortune 500 executive. If you're successful in either environment, you're doing it on the back of your strengths.

I mention this because I do not want stay-at-home parents to minimize what they do and what it takes to do it well. Organization, passion, creativity, patience and planning are a few of the strengths I observe in my wife Lisa. She displays these traits every day in her role as MFCEO (ie. "Mommy Freakin' Chief Executive Officer", a little inside joke at our house) of McDonald Corp. In all seriousness, the strengths that drive Lisa's success manifest in very diverse situations.

Consider the whole of your employment history. Look for common elements or unique circumstances that various roles afforded you. Was there a project where you were asked to take a creative lead and you nailed it? Was there an intense analytical exercise that defined a new level of excellence for you? Something a mentor you respected pointed out to you as "well done." Your employment history is rich with examples of the things you do well, these are your strengths. Look for patterns in your choices of jobs or the roles managers chose for you.

If you are young and reading this book—wow! The world is going to fall at your feet. No matter how narrow your employment experience is, if you did something successfully, you leveraged one or more of your strengths. If you work at In-N-Out Burger or Micky Ds, doesn't matter; you got the job because you displayed strengths.

Perhaps you have not started your employment journey, no fear. Look back at any reward-based activities you experienced. Perhaps you received an allowance for performing a set of chores, or had a paper route, mowed lawns or just had a lemonade stand one summer—you leveraged strengths in the process to make it happen.

• Home

I can't think of a better place to see the application of your strengths and weaknesses than at home. If you are a homemaker, if your role is to run the house, you should have no problem running through a long list of situational applications of strengths. It's very likely you have a good feel for your weaknesses as well, or at least your preferences.

If you don't have a "family dynamic" at home you may not fully understand, but I'll bet you have some idea of what it takes to manage a group of cohabiting humans with personality designs from every compass point. Before we go any further, a big tip of the hat to moms in particular. I didn't really understand what went on at home until I had the unique perspective few men get–retired with young children at home.

I thought I knew what Lisa did while I was "working." I was home about three weeks post-Fender when I was absolutely humbled by the reality I encountered. The scope and variation of tasks Lisa was dealing with every day in the act of serving our young family was monumental. Situational leadership, creativity, results focused, negotiating, analytics, organization, energy, energy (did I mention energy?), compassion, listener, teacher's heart, nutrition expert, bridge builder. With barely a thank you. Wow.

If you are working outside the home, you should still take a long hard look at your SWOT in play at home. What are you good at? What roles do you feel you are nailing and what's your secret? Does your spouse agree? Are you the peacekeeper? The vacation planner? We always gravitate toward our strengths and away from our weaknesses. What are yours at home?

APPLIED STRENGTHS ASSESSMENT TOOL

On the following pages you will find four templates. One representing each the four key areas of focus.

1. **Getting things done**

2. **Strategic energy**

3. **Bridge Building**

4. **Influencing Others.**

Each list contains sixteen words or phrases chosen to stimulate your thoughts about the application of your personal strengths.

Select those you feel you possess on a scale of 1 to 5.

• **One (1): Being just shy of a weakness,**

• **Three (3): Table stakes, but not a super power**

• **Five (5): "I got this working for me, Mr."**

Try not to overthink it the first time through. Go with your initial response for now.

I have said it before, and I am saying it again. *Objective Self-Assessment* is difficult. We all believe we understand ourselves, possesses a fair degree of self-awareness and introspective insights. We're wrong. In reality, only about ten-percent of us have pursued any type of self-awareness training. We rationalize our way out of it, "Why pursue what I already know?"

To that point, I am recommending you keep these templates

clean. You may want to scan them so you can ask others to evaluate your strengths from their perspective. It takes courage to open yourself up to a conversation about your strengths, but it is hugely beneficial if done right. Choose the right individual(s) to help you. Lend them your copy of *Rock Your Gig* or buy one for them so they understand what you are doing. A little shameless self-promotion here, but the whole point of this book is to engage others in your interpersonal journey!

We will come back to these templates at the conclusion of the *Personality Designs* portion of the book. You will have an elevated sense-of-self and this exercise may feel completely different. This is an iterative cycle. It's dynamic and evolves as we evolve.

One more time: Write it down, memorialize your perspective, make it real, visible. We will revisit your *Strengths Assessment* when we investigate the laws of attraction and the power of affirmation.

Again, I suggest you copy the following four-page *Applied Strengths Assessment* tool and keep these originals clean.

GETTING THINGS DONE

	1	2	3	4	5
Focused	○	○	○	○	○
Energized	○	○	○	○	○
Consistent	○	○	○	○	○
Organized	○	○	○	○	○
Perserverant	○	○	○	○	○
Adaptability	○	○	○	○	○
Problem Solving	○	○	○	○	○
Collaboration	○	○	○	○	○
Accountability	○	○	○	○	○
Self-Regulating	○	○	○	○	○
Urgency	○	○	○	○	○
Conscientiousness	○	○	○	○	○
Responsiveness	○	○	○	○	○
Creativity	○	○	○	○	○
Resilience	○	○	○	○	○
Decisiveness	○	○	○	○	○

STRATEGIC ENERGY

Vision	1	2	3	4	5
Analytics	1	2	3	4	5
Creative	1	2	3	4	5
Problem Solving	1	2	3	4	5
Life Learner	1	2	3	4	5
Listener	1	2	3	4	5
Ideation	1	2	3	4	5
Collaboration	1	2	3	4	5
Planning	1	2	3	4	5
Flexibility	1	2	3	4	5
Competitive	1	2	3	4	5
Relevance	1	2	3	4	5
Checkers or Chess	1	2	3	4	5
Courage	1	2	3	4	5
Risk Reward	1	2	3	4	5
Patience	1	2	3	4	5

BRIDGE BUILDING

Self Awareness   ◯   ◯   ◯   ◯   ◯
                      1   2   3   4   5

Versatility   ◯   ◯   ◯   ◯   ◯
                      1   2   3   4   5

Communication   ◯   ◯   ◯   ◯   ◯
                      1   2   3   4   5

Listening   ◯   ◯   ◯   ◯   ◯
                      1   2   3   4   5

Responsiveness   ◯   ◯   ◯   ◯   ◯
                      1   2   3   4   5

Purposeful   ◯   ◯   ◯   ◯   ◯
                      1   2   3   4   5

Humility   ◯   ◯   ◯   ◯   ◯
                      1   2   3   4   5

Esteem   ◯   ◯   ◯   ◯   ◯
                      1   2   3   4   5

Other's Needs   ◯   ◯   ◯   ◯   ◯
                      1   2   3   4   5

Versatile   ◯   ◯   ◯   ◯   ◯
                      1   2   3   4   5

Committed   ◯   ◯   ◯   ◯   ◯
                      1   2   3   4   5

Adaptability   ◯   ◯   ◯   ◯   ◯
                      1   2   3   4   5

Reinvention   ◯   ◯   ◯   ◯   ◯
                      1   2   3   4   5

Negotiations   ◯   ◯   ◯   ◯   ◯
                      1   2   3   4   5

Mediation   ◯   ◯   ◯   ◯   ◯
                      1   2   3   4   5

Non-Verbal Skills   ◯   ◯   ◯   ◯   ◯
                      1   2   3   4   5

INFLUENCING OTHERS

Expressive	◯ 1	◯ 2	◯ 3	◯ 4	◯ 5
Passionate	◯ 1	◯ 2	◯ 3	◯ 4	◯ 5
Inspirational	◯ 1	◯ 2	◯ 3	◯ 4	◯ 5
Communication	◯ 1	◯ 2	◯ 3	◯ 4	◯ 5
Empathy	◯ 1	◯ 2	◯ 3	◯ 4	◯ 5
Charisma	◯ 1	◯ 2	◯ 3	◯ 4	◯ 5
Conviction	◯ 1	◯ 2	◯ 3	◯ 4	◯ 5
Energetic	◯ 1	◯ 2	◯ 3	◯ 4	◯ 5
Listening	◯ 1	◯ 2	◯ 3	◯ 4	◯ 5
Selling	◯ 1	◯ 2	◯ 3	◯ 4	◯ 5
Consistent	◯ 1	◯ 2	◯ 3	◯ 4	◯ 5
Engaged	◯ 1	◯ 2	◯ 3	◯ 4	◯ 5
Soliciting Input	◯ 1	◯ 2	◯ 3	◯ 4	◯ 5
People Person	◯ 1	◯ 2	◯ 3	◯ 4	◯ 5
Articulate	◯ 1	◯ 2	◯ 3	◯ 4	◯ 5
On Stage	◯ 1	◯ 2	◯ 3	◯ 4	◯ 5

W.O.: WEAKNESSES & OPPORTUNITIES

No mystery here, this is everything that didn't show up on our *Applied Strengths* list, but it's so much more. Like our strengths, our weak zones don't reveal themselves until we put them to task in application. The *Rock Your Gig* process of Objective Self-Assessment further modifies the traditional SWOT analysis to combine all four elements, Strengths, Weaknesses, Opportunities and Threats into a single purposeful perspective and redefined as the *Field of Opportunity*.

The Field of Opportunity

The *Field of Opportunity* is all of our capabilities and potential playing themselves out—in the moment and in the immediate future. It's all the things we could do, if we were motivated to do them. It might include a desirable job posting at work, the potential of a new relationship, a career change, a new client or sustaining personal or professional relevance. Whether it's a business strategy or a personal goal, sizing up our capabilities and seizing the opportunity is what *growth* looks like.

Growth

Gig Rockers choose an elevated perspective on their Weaknesses and Opportunities. They see potential for *growth*. The *Field of Opportunity* is dynamic, and it can be influenced. It expands as we invest in ourselves and apply consistent, high quality energy and focus. It also contracts when we stagnate, make poor decisions or fail to sustain relevance in our rapidly moving world.

Moments of Connectivity

For those of you in leadership roles, opportunity can be hiding in plain sight. I had the privilege of working with some incredibly gifted people in my time at Fender. One of them was Mike L. Mike is the quintessential Fender product visionary—a gifted musician with the recording and performance pedigree to match; creative, curious and a style I can only describe as, "total immersion". Whatever the challenge, Mike would approach it the same way—go deep and wide and come back with a perspective that could only be born of absolute intimacy.

At the time, I was managing twenty-nine brands in FMIC's portfolio and executing a plan to unify the global marketing and artist relations divisions. You may notice I didn't say, "Leading twenty-nine brands", because I wasn't. On the leadership continuum I was "managing" many of them at best. It was culturally complicated, frustrating at times and really important.

Mike had been trying to get to me for some time. I can remember him in my doorway, observing the frenetic activity around me and backing out of the room. This happened a few times, as I recall. One afternoon Mike came in my office and asked if I had a minute, just wanted to check-in. I responded, "Thanks Mike, you sir are the least of my worries!" He offered a humble "Thanks." and turned to go. I pulled my head out of my work and asked him to sit down. As we spoke, my words started reverberating in my subconscious, "Mike, you sir are the least of my worries!" I repeated to myself. A distorted echo came back, "Mike, you sir are the bulk of my opportunity."

In the weeks, months and years ahead, Mike and I collaborated on a variety of material opportunities that drove Fender's business and our careers forward. I changed my leadership perspective and focused on the potential of my highest performers versus burning calories attempting to salvage players that were never going to deliver. Unique opportunities exist within collaboration, partnership and team. In other words, you-plus-someone-else may equal new opportunities. You plus the right "somebody" can negate a weakness and expose an opportunity.

What strengths were applied to create this situational opportunity? Always easier in retrospect, but what can we learn from it? There was so much going on at the time. What dynamics came into play for Mike to be standing in my office that day and what made me stop and say, "Sit down Mike, let's catch up." versus, "Thanks for understanding, I'm busy."?

Mindfulness? Strategic energy? Vision, patience, focus? What applied strengths created this moment in time? A moment that ultimately changed the course of a global business. What leadership hat-trick set this in motion? It wasn't our business I.Q, it was our Interpersonal Intelligence that created the spark.

Mike had been reimagining the Gretsch guitar brand and was driving a successful business. He wasn't in my office looking for help, he was there to see if he could help me. It definitely wasn't my brilliant leadership; I had put him through the same "hello and goodbye" process several times in the weeks prior. The reason I asked Mike to come back, sit down and catch up was because I saw something in his demeanor. I know Mike. I know his body language. I know these things because I genuinely care about meeting his needs.

And I saw that I wasn't meeting Mike's needs. It wasn't some inspired vision hovering over me, like divine intervention or strategic mana from heaven. I could see in his demeanor it was time to take it to the bridge. I put my agenda away and sat down to listen, to give Mike the time he needed. Remember, that wasn't easy for me either! My personality can be completely self-absorbed when I'm in, "Get results now" mode (Lisa could write a book on the subject). It's a Strength and a Weakness I am still learning to harness.

The spark of self-awareness created an interpersonal moment and a connection was made. From there anything can happen, potential becomes redefined. This is why I am so compelled to share the *Rock Your Gig* philosophy. Objective self-awareness, continual improvement, reinvention—you don't have to master these things for them to contribute to your personal and professional success. Just activating them moves you forward.

Collaboration and Team Engagement
What ultimately came from that initial conversation was significant. It didn't all come pouring out on the table that afternoon, but it flowed and gained momentum for months. Dominoes started falling; cascading connectivity spreading to others. Interpersonal energy is amazing. No fire starts without a spark to ignite it and connecting effectively with purposeful behavior throws a lot of sparks.

Yes, its chaos theory, but much like the weather, we can forecast sunny days with some degree of accuracy. Throw enough sparks and something is going to catch fire. Throw no sparks? Well, you know.

Unraveling what seemed like random awesomeness reveals a progression that begins with Interpersonal Effectiveness. Once people come together and focus, the rest begins to feel organic. It's finding our way to that initial connection that can break the status quo. This is what performing like rock star is all about. Let's take a synthesized look at this, "Least of my worries." case study.

- **Interpersonal Awareness created a moment.**
- **Building bridges created elevated connectivity.**
- **Applied Strengths were aligned.**
- **Weaknesses mitigated through collaboration.**
- **Collaboration revealed strategic opportunities.**
- **Reinvention neutralized threats and sustains relevance.**

T.: THREATS

Just because I'm paranoid doesn't mean people aren't after me. Classic stuff. I always thought Threats was such an aggressive term. I guess it's not bad if you consider the options; Strengths, Weaknesses, Opportunities and Perils? Let's just stick with Threats.

Strategic planning considers threats across many variables; regulatory threats, competitive threats, costs, changes in market demand, people, competitive innovation—the list goes on and on. Eventually, every business will deal with threats of some kind. Our view can be so internally focused, we don't see what's happening around us, or worse, we discount it, rationalize its lack of impact and keep going.

By the late '90s, innovation started finding its way into the surprisingly conventional electric guitar market. You may not be aware that the majority of pro-level guitarists you see performing on stage, or listen to on your device, use guitar amplifiers powered by 1940s vacuum tube technology. With a few exceptions, most of the guitars themselves are designs that originated in the 1950s and '60s. The music has changed immensely, but the instrument in your hands is pretty much the same. Why? Those old tools are supported by a massive and highly influential body of work that used those guitars and amps in their creation. But again, that "comfort and illusion" that I spoke of in the Spirit of Reinvention chapter creeps into the picture.

Players continued to resist change on the instruments specifically, but were more open to innovation in the signal path, or everything after the electronic signal is transmitted out of the instrument towards the amplifier. Customers, many of whom are serious hobbyists, didn't have the resources, expertise or space to replicate the systems used by their guitar heroes. Only the most committed to the "pursuit of tone" would take this on.

Threats start small. Initially, you can barely see them, they are easy to discount and ignore—until they're not. I had a front row seat for this movie entitled, *"The Rise of Digital Amplification."* It was an important and costly lesson I was about to learn.

We sat in the sound room, arms crossed in strategic defense mode, "These (competitor's) amps sound like ass!" commented one of our senior engineers. The sentiment was shared by the amplifier product and marketing teams, which I was leading at the time. The amp in front of us was the Line 6 Flextone, the first commercially viable digital guitar amplifier. It was the brain child of innovative designer Marcus Ryle who brought his keyboard digital-modeling expertise from Oberheim synthesizers and applied it as a solution for guitarists. The solution was "digital modeling"—a replication of classic vacuum tube guitar sounds replicated by computer-like digital circuitry.

The product solved a ton of problems for guitarists. You didn't need those "old tools" (multiple vintage amps and an effects-board with 20 pedals) to achieve the tones originally used to create all the sounds heard in modern music. It was an all-in-one, easy to transport amplifier that absolutely sounded like ass (even I agreed on that point), but again, solved a ton of guitarist's problems. The only people that didn't think the amps sounded bad, or didn't care, where all the consumers that bought them. And they bought a lot of them. If they sounded so bad why were they turning in stores?

Pride Comes Before the Fall

We were so successful at this point I believe our collective egos got in the way. We also found it difficult to focus on one area of our line. No one in the industry was effectively doing it, but Fender was trying to design and sell electric guitars and basses, acoustic guitars, guitar, bass and keyboard amplification, pro audio and sound reinforcement gear. It was like painting the Golden Gate bridge—by the time we finished it was rusty and time to start again. Though we were the market leader in sales, our innovation energy was spread too thin.

What threats did we miss, ignore or rationalize as unimportant? Self-awareness can be just as difficult for businesses as it is for individuals. Where did our process let us down? The answers to those questions crossed many borders.

We didn't see this new competitor as a threat, or the emerging segment of nontraditional amplifiers as an *opportunity*. We were blindsided by the consumer interest due to internal *weaknesses* in our strategic planning processes and perspectives. We were laser focused on one thing, *our Strengths*.

This dynamic is not exclusive to businesses. Similar scenarios are played out on a personal level every day. This is the value of an internally focused SWOT. We need a formal process to ensure we give our Objective Self-Assessment the attention it deserves and to establish a baseline of effectiveness to improve upon.

THREATS to CONSIDER

• Competition

We all compete at some level, in some way. We compete for the affection of another (wink, wink, nudge, nudge), we compete for jobs, recognition and accolades. We even compete with ourselves in an effort to grow. Competitive threats on the horizon can be and should be, powerful motivators if we choose to compete with them.

• Relevance

The loss of relevance can be a threat to individuals and businesses as well. We must sustain a degree of personal relevance to compete and maintain technological and social relevance. Sustaining personal relevance and avoiding the threat of obsolescence needs to be viewed through the lens of opportunity (as opposed to fear). How many people got left behind when the information age came barreling in and evolving every two minutes? In the print industry alone, the skills of old school typesetters, cut-and-paste layout artists, color separators and air brush photo re-touchers are no longer relevant.

Much like the information age, the machine age is creating a graveyard of obsolete job skills. It's a threat for many individuals. If you see this on the horizon, make a change if at all possible. Don't just admire the problem; create a plan to sustain your relevance in an evolving field or enter a new one. I think about this every time I go to the grocery store. The check-out clerks are dwindling. The new job is fixing the self-scanners when they break!

- **Health, Pain and Pleasure**

Here's a threat that is really easy to ignore and can create problems far more disastrous than sustaining relevance. Your health. When it comes to Objective Self-Assessment, start here and be brutally honest. As a Threat, your health must be taken seriously. We usually wait until something breaks down before we are willing to acknowledge the threat related to our health. We become victims at that point, it's just so much easier ...or so we think. Classic Pain and Pleasure dynamic. Once the pain eclipses the pleasure, we make a move, but it doesn't need to be that way.

Remember, your physical well-being is part of the Ecosystem of You. It's a big part. When we are considering internal threats, this has to be highlighted. The topic of our health often gets the big, "Yeah, I know, I know, but..." and the excuses start materializing. Yes, your health has a whole lot to do with your success, fulfillment and happiness.

- **Stress Management**

Stress is a killer. It kills our fun; it kills our energy. For me, it killed everything but my appetite (apparently). All joking aside, this should be seen as a very serious threat. It can build in a linear fashion, we may not even notice it, until we do and that's usually a little too late. Stress manifests itself in so many ways. If you are relating to this right now, make this your main area of focus. Get strategic, get deep, get smart, get help and get out from under whatever is tying you up.

My recovery from brain surgery gave me the opportunity for personal reflection, as you can imagine. I'll tell you all about it someday. I performed a personal post-mortem on my lifestyle over the past five years. Stage three cancer will make a man introspective and spiritual. I needed Lisa's help to keep it objective and it took quite some time to really begin to understand the role stress had played in my current situation.

When I retired from Fender, I saw another piece of the puzzle and I started to put the bigger picture together. It actually took months for the inertia of leadership stress to dissipate. Even though I had taken off the yoke of responsibility, I still felt the churn. Then it started to pass. I didn't understand how stressed I was ...until I wasn't.

What I learned is you can live an unsustainable lifestyle for years, but ultimately it is just that—unsustainable. Eventually something will breakdown. It's not necessarily our health; it could be an important relationship or missed opportunity. In my case, it was the combination of self-induced stress and a total disregard for the balance and health of my ecosystem that brought me down. It was a threat I didn't respect or fear, and it completely blindsided me. Not only did I not see it as a threat, I didn't have a purposeful strategy or belief system to help me mitigate it. Don't let stress go unattended—it's absolutely an internal threat to be recognized and respected.

- **Interpersonal Blindness**

Saving the best for last. You can have everything imaginable working for you; talent, knowledge, experience, incredibly good looks–the complete package– but you can be brought down by something I call, interpersonal blindness.) It is a threat we rarely see until we see the impact, even the wreckage and havoc, it can wreak. We rarely see the root cause but will instead have a misguided tendency to define the root cause as "other people."

You know the clichés, "He can't get out of his own way." or, "She has no people skills." They tell the story of an absence of self-awareness. What's really interesting, is when you meet self-aware people you notice they are also aware of other's needs. Believe me, "It takes one, to know one", and I've been one.

• Internally Focused Threats

Once again, this internally focused threat can be situational. We can be in-tune with the needs of our boss and not the needs of our spouse. We can be connecting at home, but not at work. The power of Interpersonal Awareness and Objective Self-Assessment is that any energy invested realizes amazing outcomes. Strengths are enhanced and threats become opportunities; for growth, for captivating discovery, wellness and joy. The fact that you are reading *Rock Your Gig* shouts that you see the value in Interpersonal Effectiveness. Take a survey of your relationships. Are there any that are at risk? Any that pose a significant threat? Document these thoughts in your Personal SWOT and let's outline and start developing plans to eliminate or minimize interpersonal threats.

For now, simply record your thoughts with the data from your personal SWOT. Be specific about areas of interpersonal risk or threats. As we work through other elements of the Ecosystem of You, we will have an elevated perspectives and new tools to help navigate or eliminate interpersonal threats.

Next Steps

Give yourself adequate time to complete this first draft of your Objective Self-Assessment. The internal SWOT should feel like a journey as much as an exercise. Don't let perfection be the enemy of progress. It's more important to complete the entire SWOT than to optimize any one element. Let it sit while you read on in RYG. The themes are all connected so you won't lose your focus or momentum.

Seek outside input via the Strengths template if at all possible.

Come back to your notes when new perspectives hit you. Think about the case studies offered – are there parallels in your professional or personal life?

Arrange the SWOT data into an expression of the *Field of Opportunity* at play in your life.

Where are your strengths optimized?

When are you happiest?

What scares you and what could change your fears?

What is the cost?

What do I need?

What can be done?

Stay away from the *Why*, and stick to *What* questions—What can be done? What is the cost? What do I need? Using the interpersonal SWOT to ask and answer *What* questions moves us forward, while *Why* questions effectively press "pause" as we attempt to answer unanswerable questions. And finally, if this isn't particularly fun, you're probably doing it right. This is what separates those who came to rock—the willingness to do what needs to be done, to ask and answer, "What is possible?"

S.W.O.T REWIND

Objective Self-Assessment

Self-assessment is tricky. Seeing ourselves objectivity is the challenge. The process can be awkward at first.

Internalized SWOT: (page 70)

The *Rock Your Gig* philosophy modifies the traditional SWOT to focus all four dimensions internally.

Context and Environment: (page 71)

Strengths and weaknesses are situational and manifest differently depending on the context and environment.

Seek Input: (page 72)

Consider soliciting input from a trusted source. Use the trigger templates for this purpose.

Applied Strengths: (page 72)

The four categories of Applied Strengths are...

1. **Getting Things Done**
2. **Strategic Energy**
3. **Bridge Building**
4. **Influencing Others**

Actualizing Strengths: (page 73)

Strengths are not actualized until they are activated, applied and curated.

Where to look for Applied Strengths: (page 74)

Search for examples of *Applied Strengths* by using a thee category formula

- **Early Life Equity**
- **Educational Journey**
- **Employment History**
- **Home**

We always gravitate toward our strengths and away from our weaknesses. What are yours at home?

Field of Opportunity: (page 82)
Rock Your Gig makes a second modification to the traditional SWOT design, it combines all internally focused dimensions into one perspective, we call the *Field of Opportunity*. It is all the potential playing out in the moment and on the immediate horizon. It expands as we invest in ourselves, apply consistent, high quality energy and focus.

Growth: (page 84)
Gig rockers see both opportunity and weakness as potential for growth.

Moments of Connectivity: (page 84)
Elevated *Interpersonal Awareness* creates moments of connectivity. This spark starts a chain reaction of potential.

Collaboration and Team Engagement: (page 86)
These strengths offset weaknesses and expose opportunity.

Threats: (page 87)
Consider threats across these themes:

Competition	**Stress Management**
Relevance	**Interpersonal Blindness**
Health	

Health, Pain and Pleasure: (page 90)
When the pain eclipses the pleasure, we seem to be open to change.

Internally Focused Threats: (page 92)
These can be hard to see, and easy to discount. We often assume a victim mentality regarding threats and weaknesses.

CHAPTERS 1-5 REVIEW

1. The Spirit of Reinvention

We understand and believe in the willingness to reimagine our lives. It is powerful and is ours for the taking–if we have the motivation and courage.

2. The Ecosystem of You

We all function in an integrated and interdependent environment we refer to as the Ecosystem of "you". The health status of the ecosystem is positively and negatively affected by our Physical, Emotional and Spiritual Health

The perspectives presented in *Rock Your Gig* are all elements of a diverse and dynamic ecosystem. The Ecosystem of "you". is the independent, yet connected, collection of our beliefs, strengths, weaknesses, personality design, wellness and balance—all in harmony and working together... or not. There is no silver bullet solution that delivers predictable career progression. It may include the seven habits of highly contagious winners, but it's chaos theory at best. It isn't the top ten keys to success, it's the compounded impact of everything we do with consistency, honor and energy.

3. Balance in the Ecosystem of You

We determined that the best process to evaluate the status of our ecosystem is to survey and seek a higher level of Life Balance. *Rock Your Gig* takes an integrated perspective on life balance.

The first step in restructuring an unbalanced ecosystem is to snap out of the ignorance of the status quo. Keanu Reeves made a fun movie and, in it, an unimaginably bold observation, *"We are all asleep, living in a destructive yet comfortable illusion."*

4. Objective Self-Awareness

This is the essential understanding of our Strengths, Weaknesses, Opportunities and Threats. It defines our Field of Opportunity.

5. S.W.O.T. Analysis

Applying the tools in this section can be a challenge. Be objective and honest with yourself and seek the input of others to arrive at the best results.

All of this ets the table for what is coming next; **Personality Designs.**

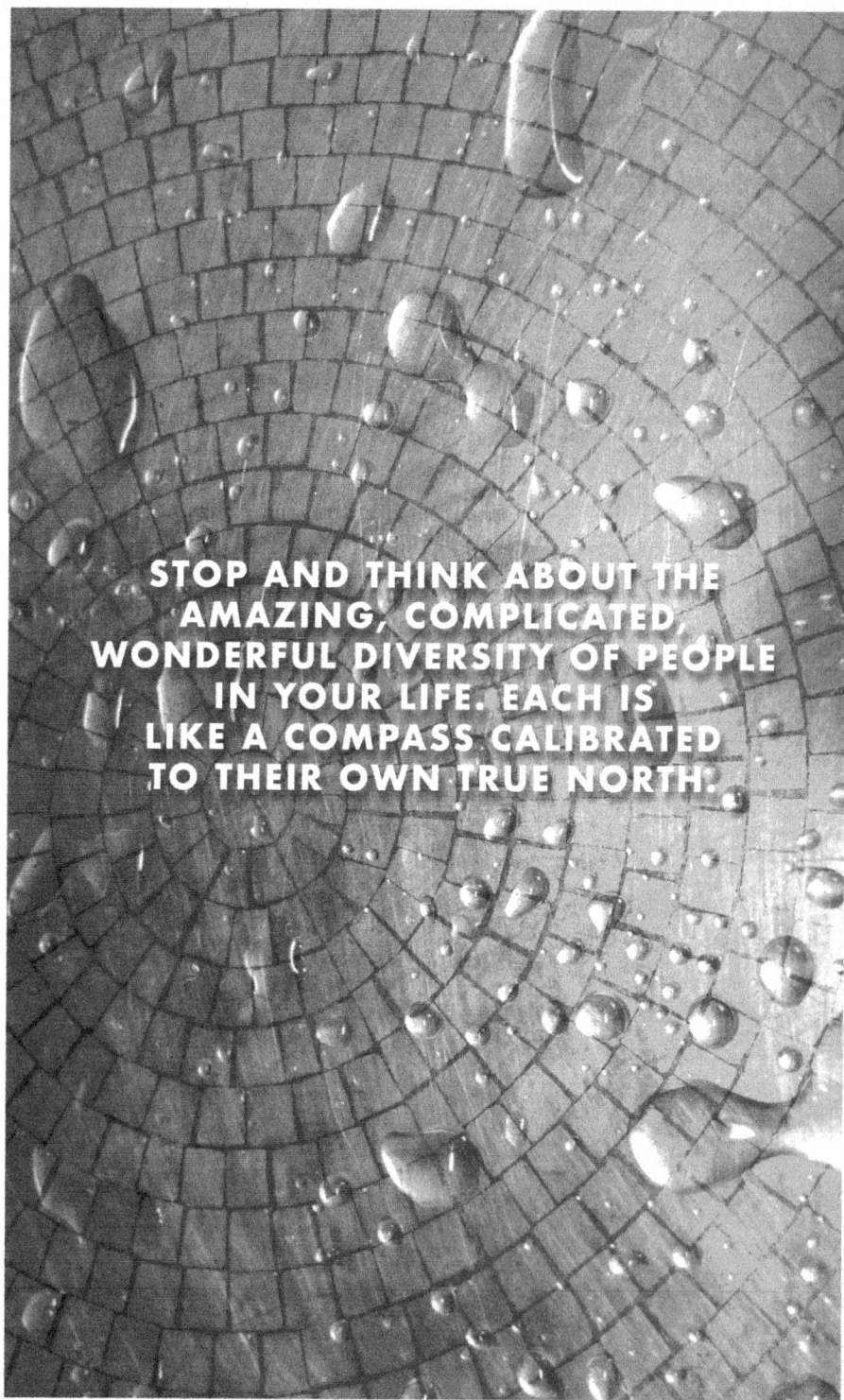

STOP AND THINK ABOUT THE
AMAZING, COMPLICATED,
WONDERFUL DIVERSITY OF PEOPLE
IN YOUR LIFE. EACH IS
LIKE A COMPASS CALIBRATED
TO THEIR OWN TRUE NORTH.

CHAPTER 6

PERSONALITY DESIGNS

CHAPTER 6.

PERSONALITY DESIGNS

Stop for just a moment. Stop and think about your family or the people closest to you. Stop and think about each individual. The way they dress, the way they speak, the things they say (and don't say). Think about the interplay between your parents and your own marriage or relationship. Think about your kids. Do you describe their individual traits as "night and day?"

Personality Design is a tool to help us understand the unique needs and preferences of others as well as our own. It gives us the ability to close gaps with others and create positive connectivity.

Now think about your workplace, home or office gig. Think about the people you interact with; the guy in HR (you know the one I'm talking about), the gal in accounting that's never at her desk but always has fresh baked goods, the super friendly loud guy behind the cash register, the friendly IT guy that doesn't make you feel stupid.

Now, think about your favorite television series, HBO or Netflix film. Think about the ensemble cast; Joey, Rachel, Chandler and Phoebe, Spock, Kirk, Bones and Scotty. Now put them in a medieval castle and give them swords and unpronounceable names for the sake of relevance.

Stop and think about the amazing, complicated, wonderful diversity of the people in your life. Each like a compass calibrated to their own True North. This is the beautiful, magical and sometimes frustrating nature of "us" and our world.

Understanding this breadth of diversity, what makes us think, for even a passing moment of delusional upbeat contemplation, that a one-size-fits-all approach to interpersonal encounters is going to be effective? In the midst of this fragmented, custom-embroidered, personalized world, why would we actually think it's effective to deal with everybody the same way?

I'll tell you why. We don't even think about it. We do "us", and that's about it. "But!" the crowd yelled, "Us being "us" is what's real man, it's authentic, it's who I am!" No, it's not. It's who you think you are. If you want to find out who you are, you have to ask other people. "Dude, man, don't screw up my theories with facts, please." I'm sorry, I know it's not an easy pill to swallow.

You will recall, almost 90% of your acquaintances, friends and family believe they have a degree of self-awareness and only about 10% actually do. They believe they understand how they are perceived, and, typically, they are wrong. If this is you, objective self-assessment and external input are the best tools to start this fire.

Personality Designs gives us a key to unlock the motivations, needs and behaviors of others, and how to begin to think about meeting others' needs first. When we use this knowledge thoughtfully with grace and sincerity, we create moments of positive connectivity. Interactions that expand *The Field of Opportunity*.

History

During the 1950s and 1960s, there was an explosion of interest and perspectives on the human journey of self-awareness. At one end of the '60s spectrum, you had the pop psychology of Tom Wolfe's *Electric Kool-Aid Acid Test*[15]. If you recall, Tom and his buddy Ken Kesey encouraged us to find inner awareness through LSD (uh, don't worry about the hole it burns in your brain). Carlos Castaneda the author of *A Separate Reality*[16] promised to enlighten us through his conversations with Yaqui Indian shaman Don Juan and some powerful psychotropic drugs. I know because I bought into all of this.

In contrast, studies like those of industrial psychologists,

Dr. David Merrill and Roger Reid focused on predicting the outcomes of human capital[17]. This landmark study is the foundation of the *Rock Your Gig Personality Designs* approach. Your personality design drives your social demeanor, or the behaviors we express when we are interacting with others.

The research was focused on behaviorism and behavior characteristics. Participants were given a list of 150 adjectives that reflected degrees of Responsiveness, Assertiveness and Versatility. The frame of reference grew out of work by Robert Blake and Jane Mouton and their management grid model which helped synthesize the view.

Assertiveness

What eventually emerged was a matrix defined by two continuums. Along the horizontal plane is the degree of Assertiveness which is defined by the extent people will go to influence others. The most assertive designs are represented to the right, while assertiveness decreases along the horizontal plane to the left.

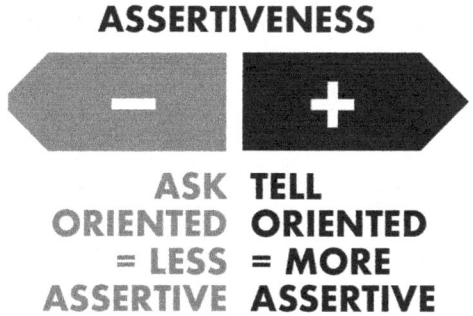

6a. Assertiveness Continuum

The assertiveness continuum is further defined by two key characteristic behaviors, *Ask* oriented designs, and *Tell* oriented designs. It's a measure of *how aggressively we attempt to influence an outcome and the kinds of behaviors we use to make it happen.* Although ask-oriented people are less assertive, they are no less effective. Sometimes, a well-timed whisper can be more effective than shouting.

My wife Lisa and I are on opposite ends of the Assertiveness scale. Of course we are, opposites attract, right? Yin and Yang. I'm on the *Tell* side of the assertiveness continuum. I purposefully march through life convinced I know where I'm going, pretty convinced I know where you should be going too, making great time, all according to plan. My behavior is more assertive than some and less than others. Compared to my seven-year old daughter Charlee, she makes me look lost and indecisive!

Lisa is on the *Ask* side of assertiveness, along with our son Micah. She's not going to speak over you, interrupt or dominate the conversation, cut in front of you in line, or honk at you on the highway. Her personality isn't designed that way. Keep in mind...

Assertiveness is only a behavioral characteristic. It's our method of influencing a situational outcome. It's how we sell our point of view.

She doesn't need to be overtly assertive to get things done, she has other traits that propel her amazingly fulfilled and positive life. She doesn't need to be assertive to be successful. Neither do you. You do need to understand your personality design and those of others.

We will learn more about assertive designs and Ask and Tell oriented personalities in the pages ahead. If you are an Assertive or if you are living with an Assertive Tell oriented individual, then standby because there is lots of good information and tools ahead. For now, with a pencil not a pen, start plotting where people you know and love fall on the Ask or Tell line. Think about people you know and love. Which direction do they lean—more or less assertive? There are nuances to come, but for now, just look for the bold examples of Ask and Tell behaviors.

Responsiveness
Along the vertical plane, perpendicular to the assertive horizontal, is the degree of Responsiveness, or the measure of emotional control we exhibit in response to external stimuli.

(The top of the scale represents less responsiveness or more emotional control. As you travel south, emotional responsiveness increases and control decreases. Responsiveness translates to the behavioral profiles of *Task* or *People* orientation.

RESPONSIVENESS

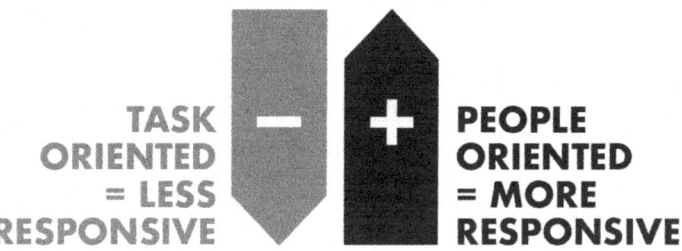

TASK
ORIENTED
= LESS
RESPONSIVE

PEOPLE
ORIENTED
= MORE
RESPONSIVE

6b. Responsiveness Continuum

Examples should come to mind fairly easily. Who do you know that is comfortable expressing themselves emotionally? You might occasionally need to call an "over-sharing violation" on them, right? TMI! Who do you know that is emotionally locked down? They may have the same *level* of feelings, they just don't share them. Think Batman or Clint Eastwood as Dirty Harry.

When someone calls, text or emails you, does the conversation start with "How's the family?" Or do they go right to the job at hand? "How's that chemo treatin' ya man?" Do you spend uncomfortable, awkward time with people stopping by your desk when you're buried up to your blood-shot eyes, and want to talk about …stuff? Forever? Don't hurt their feelings, they love you.

With these two axes in place, you begin to see the dynamic range of behavioral patterns or *Personality Designs*. It should be stimulating new thoughts and elevating your sensitivity to the behaviors you observe in others. It's hard to believe there is some order to all this chaos but there is. Start with these two simple lenses; Ask or Tell / People or Project. Look around at the people closest to you. Don't formalize your perspective yet. It's early, there's more to come. Do start to chart people along the two axes. Don't overthink it. Start with Assertive Personality Designs, we are always easy to see—or hear.

How about you? Where do you think you fall on these two continuums? Are you Ask oriented? It doesn't mean you're weak, it means your personality design is less assertive, more Ask oriented. Do you love people—c'mon, a little? Are you a social butterfly, or Lone Wolf McQuade? I understand Chuck Norris doesn't personally endorse feelings. Time to put the X and Y together to form the **Personality Designs Möbius**.

IT'S WHO WE ARE AND HOW
WE FIT TOGETHER AS
HUMAN BEINGS. IT'S BEAUTIFUL,
IT'S HUMAN AND IT'S REAL.

PERSONALITY DESIGN DESIGN MÕBIUS

∞

CHAPTER 7.

PERSONALITY DESIGN MÖBIUS

The *Personality Designs Möbius* is formed by the intersection of the two axes of Assertiveness and Responsiveness. From this perspective, four distinct personality designs are revealed. In *Rock Your Gig* terminology, they are classified as, *The "4Cs" Personality Designs Möbius.*

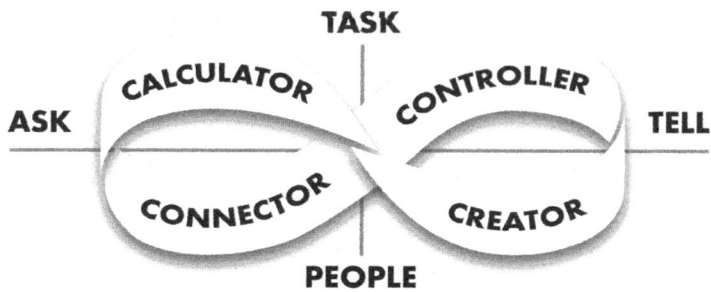

7a. The Personality Design Möbius

The "4Cs" Personality Design Möbius

Here is our first leap of faith. We have taken the entire scope of human behavioral diversity and reduced it to four personality designs. Yes, I know it's hard to believe something so simple can offer meaningful insight. Stick with me and I'll get you there, it's amazingly on the money.

The 4C terminology is a unique *Rock Your Gig* perspective. I selected each of the four superhero-sounding monikers specifically to be bold triggers, to illuminate and reflect the core behavioral characteristics of each of the four personality designs. Read them all positively, with an upbeat tone! They are superpowers, unique gifts bestowed upon each of us. These names are not personality indictments, they are a celebration! The science behind the möbius is deep. *It doesn't serve us as Gig Rockers to overthink it to any great degree.* However, I am a fan of curiosity and knowledge, so let me share enough to validate the work.

Over the past fifty-years, millions of individuals have participated in behavioral characteristics studies in support of Merrill and Reid's groundbreaking work. The behavioral sciences have sustained an interest in the perspectives it offered. Organizations have rallied around *Social Styles*[18] as an area of study. The result is a remarkable collection of substantiating work supporting the relevance of the *Personality Designs* model as a tool to help navigate interpersonal waters.

One of the questions people frequently ask is, "Which Personality Design has the most people?" When I asked this question,, I found the answer in the Social Styles Handbook. And when I did, I almost tipped-over ...again. After studying millions of participants, this is what the data revealed:

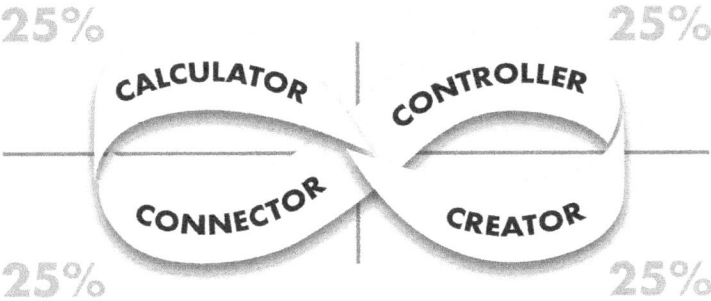

7b. Personality design distribution

That's right, after fifty years of solid research, millions of controlled, scientifically sound interviews, and the distribution is, say it with me, "Absolutely even." You expect me to believe this is just a random outcome? It can't be that rigid, seriously? It can't be a random coincidence, it's too perfect, too functional, too purposeful. It's an interpersonal crystal.

Thus, *Personality Designs* was born, because it must be by design. It's who we are and how we fit together as human beings. It's beautiful, it's human and its real. No need to get hung-up on this, but wow, you have to admit it's probably not the outcome you were expecting. I know I was shocked. The quantum geometry of our world is stunning when it reveals itself.

FIGHT OR FLIGHT

Behavioral Tendencies Under Stress

English punk rockers *The Clash* were spelling it out for us when Mick Jones delivered his passionate and somewhat ominous request for clarity in, "*Should I Stay or Should I Go?*"[19]. If you are going to make a passionate plea for clarity, do it at a 115 BPM —punk rock and the sympathetic nervous system, it doesn't get much better!

What on earth does "fight or flight" have to do with *Personality Designs*? EVERYTHING. We all have an autonomic nervous system, it's part of the standard package. It's the Operations Officer and the Information Officer combined. It makes sure all our systems are running correctly, and have the biochemical resources we need, where and when we need them. This all happens unbeknownst to us, which is probably ok because it seems incredibly complicated.

There is a team reporting to the Autonomic Department known as the Sympathetic Nervous System. This team is stationed in our spinal column and stand at the ready to detect any threats coming our way. It's essentially an early warning defense system.

When the system detects a potential threat, it sends a complete report to the Head of Autonomics requesting support. The team in Autonomics places warehouse transfer orders for Adrenaline to be delivered immediately. Our heartbeat increases, we feel a little tension in our spine as the reports keep coming in from the Sympathetic team in the field. Our palms get sweaty, the tension in our neck increases. It hits a tipping point and… it's on, or you're gone.

Here's the thing, this is all happening on a continuum. That word again. There is a whole lot happening in the gray area between black and white. The fight or flight response isn't just activated in life and death scenarios, it's always on. Ever diligent, it activates when we are under stress of any kind. We can learn to recognize it, even regulate it to a degree, but its freaking *automatic*, don't forget. We might not even be emotionally aware we are fighting or fleeing. I would venture a guess we aren't aware the majority of the time.

Self-aware people understand this dynamic. They know they must be emotionally intelligent and aware, even if it's not an organic strength of their *Personality Design*. Yes, that's you *Controller*! Don't laugh *Calculator*, you're in the same club. As task responsiveness increases our emotional control increases. When we are in *deep* task mode, we can be completely unaware of the tension we are creating in others. Conversely, a lack of urgency and commitment can create tension in task-oriented individuals. It goes both ways. You know what they say about complicated people? You're one of them.

THE RULES
Before we go any further, let's set some very clear ground rules and dismantle key misconceptions about the *Personality Designs Möbius*. This is a covenant, seriously. Thanks.

• It's Not How People Feel
It's not what is inside them, it's how they behave in different situations, under different stimuli. It is *not* a reflection of peoples' hearts, or how deeply they love and care.

• It Has No Influence on Leadership Potential
It's very easy to jump to the conclusion that, "The more assertive people are, the more likely they are to be in leadership roles." This is absolutely untrue. *Leaders are effective because they understand people, not because they are assertive.*

• It Has No Influence On Success

It doesn't matter where you fall on the 4C möbius, success is an equal opportunity blessing. As leaders, successful individuals understand the needs of others and meet them.

• It Doesn't Answer, "Why?"

The question never came up in the research. Don't go there. None of this is why people do things. It is simply peoples' interpersonal comfort zones. I believe it was Confucius who said, "A little physiology is like a little karate, you might get your butt kicked." It might have been Chuck Norris.

• Seek To Understand Others First

That's the whole *Rock Your Gig* philosophy. Understand their needs, understand where you are and build a bridge to cross the span. It starts with understanding others first.

• Don't Try To Plot Yourself

We absolutely need to figure that out, but you have to solicit the input of others to get an accurate read. We do not see our behaviors as others do. You do not see yourself as others see you.

• Don't Over Analyze

Take a generalized approach. Think of it as a navigational aid in rougher waters. Sometimes we have to make a few quick assumptions, and course adjust as we go.

• Don't Negatively Categorize

Don't use someone's personality design to create a negative mental image. People aren't good or bad because of their personality design. We are all perfect in our design.

• It's Situational

We respond differently in different situations; for example, our assertiveness can increase with confidence and diminish in unfamiliar circumstances. Be careful not to create blanket solutions, each situation needs its own perspective.

Meet the Band

In the following pages, we will explore each of the "Fab-Four" personality designs in greater detail. We'll look at *Motivators, Priorities, Preferences* and *Needs* and identify stress-inducing behaviors as well as more enriching paths. Communication is far more than the words we choose; identifying and reading nonverbal behavior is key as well.

What happens when things heat up? like the Bowie / Queen song, when we're *Under Pressure*[20], and our behavior takes a turn in *fight or flight* mode? Do we dig in, or acquiesce? Are we unknowingly the source of friction?

Most importantly, how do we use this understanding of others' needs to create moments of positive connectivity that fuel the ecosystem and expand the field of opportunity? This is the goal.

THE CONTROLLER IS AN ENGINE
THAT POWERS PROJECTS.
THEIR TASK ORIENTATION, ENERGY
AND FOCUS KEEPS US ON TRACK,
ACCOUNTABLE AND DELIVERS RESULTS.

CHAPTER 8

THE CONTROLLER

CHAPTER 8.

THE CONTROLLER

DEFINING BEHAVIORAL CHARACTERISTICS

The *Controller* personality design is a great place to start. Their *Tell / Assertive* style paired to a Task / Responsive orientation is usually easy to see, hear and feel. "Honey, do these slacks make me look pushy?" *Controllers* get things done in a world of distractions. They are focused and wired for results, getting the anticipated results, on time, on budget and on plan. Getting it done isn't necessarily getting it done perfectly, after all, "Perfection is the enemy of progress." Based on the circumstances, a 96% is great! But hey, we will absolutely hit it if possible, I mean we still have time, let's rally and nail it."

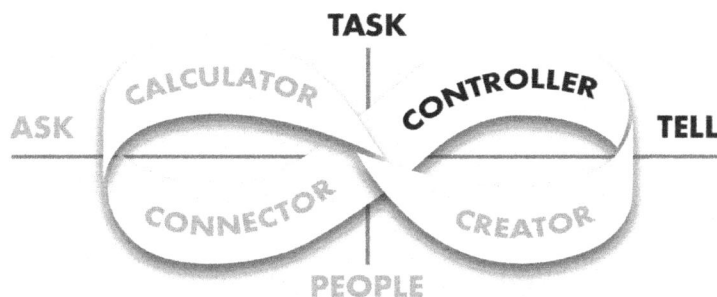

8a. The Controller: TASK-oriented, TELL-assertive

When *Controllers* say, "We can get this done.", they mean the team can get this done with the *Controller's* oversight and leadership. Their preferred work style is independent, and they prefer to initiate, oversee, and monitor results.

Controllers are direct in their communications style. They get to the point quickly. They are often opinionated and have the confidence of their convictions. Their speech is usually faster paced and unemotional. They typically display a laminated demeanor: they are put together well. They are hard-working, self-motivated and energized. Results matter.

We were moving into our "forever house". Footnote here: I had totally bought into the idea of, "your last home" and thought we were at that intersection, when the Board of Directors asked us to move the front office from Arizona to California. Our "forever house" turned out to be the one right before the other four "forever houses". But to get back to the story, Lisa and I began the joyful process of moving into our "forever house". True to my *Controller* design I was kicking butt and taking names. My to-do list was evaporating before my eyes. I'm not sure I would call my approach "joyful", but "purposeful", yes. I unpacked a blue ceramic sun and hug it on our patio fireplace and moved on to the next task. As I walked away, I heard two shattering sounds. The first, was the blue sun lying in a heap of shards which had promptly fallen due to my hurried installation, and the second was Lisa's heart breaking when she turned to see what had happened. I didn't know the intrinsic value it had to her until I mishandled it. My, "You can't make an omelet without breaking a few blue suns." humorous attempt to ease her sadness wasn't the best fit in this situation. I felt emotionally clumsy, because I was. Everything isn't a task to be checked off the list. Despite my instincts, some things require a bit more care, a bit more sensitivity.

• **The Controller** likes to win a little more than the average bear. As our daughter once reminded us when we counseled her on placing too much importance on winning, "It's about participation honey, it doesn't matter who wins", we offered. Her response cleared up any misconceptions we had when she told us passionately, "It matters to me!" Winning matters to controllers.

• **The Controller** is confident and capable, they lean in on challenges. They often display the courage and energy to take on tasks others find too difficult. Their focus and natural ability to plan and manage workflow fuels their higher productivity.

• **The Controller** is already bored and wishes we would just get on with it.

• **The Controller** manages their emotional output closely and wishes you would too. They possess all the same feelings as non-controllers, but they don't expose or share them readily. All elevated relationships are based on trust and comfort.

• **The Controller** is not going to get to trust and comfort without credibility. If you don't "have it" in their eyes, they're not going to feel comfortable trading emotional chops (I'm not even sure what Robin really knows about Batman.)

• **The Controller** doesn't naturally possess great listening skills. No problem, I was just saying controllers don't listen well. They are Tell oriented. And while they enjoy new challenges, they don't readily accept new perspectives; they need to be pressure tested for validity and credibility before they buy in.

• **The Controller** would like us all to know they don't like to waste time, so please... "Can we just stop wasting time?"

• **The Controller** is an engine that powers projects. Their Task orientation, energy and focus keep us on track, accountable and delivers results.

• **The Controller** is quick to respond to problems and is decisive.

CONTROLLER DESIGN UNDER STRESS

The *Controller,* like the *Creator,* is on the right side of the grid. East of the meridian and on the high end of Assertiveness. It is a continuum, so they plot at various points within the *Controller* design. Most of us are not pure examples of personality designs: we have dominant designs and secondary designs. For example, I am a dominant *Creator* with a healthy dose of *Controller.* It was my creative energy and my ability to rally enthusiasm that propelled my career at Fender and fuels my successes today. Certainly, years of designing and developing products, delivering growth, hiring and firing influenced me. I'm not a *Controller,* but I play one on TV. I'm not saying it's a stretch, just that it's not my dominant design.

Our secondary design is always going to be adjacent. You're not going to be a dominant *Controller* with a secondary *Connector* design. That's jumping the assertiveness scale beyond reason. People might call you "*Sybil*."[21] In other words, you may display stress behaviors consistent with two designs. It's not black and white, i.e. you are a Controller therefore... it's more like *Fifty Shades of Grey* (...without the disturbing sexual stuff. Ok, maybe it's nothing like *Fifty Shades of Grey*)

• **The Controller** will stand their ground under stress. They are ready for a fight. It's a war of few words and a lot of nonverbal messaging.

• **The Controller** doesn't like to be second-guessed and can respond quickly and sharply to criticism. Their directness under pressure can be alarming.

• **The Controller** will default to autocratic behaviors when their influence isn't getting it done. Position power is quickly leveraged to restore order.

• **The Controller** has a low tolerance for feelings and attitudes. As emotional energy increases, they start shutting down and other"s credibility is lost.

• **The Controller** under pressure will stop listening. They operate from a position of I know, versus "I feel", "I think", or I" like."

• **The Controller** is comfortable with conflict and typically has a thick skin, after all, to them, "It's not personal."

• **The Controller** can become very impatient under stress. Their natural high degree of urgency can become a hyper-focused, aggressive judgmental attack.

• **The Controller** can be intimidating under duress.

Every individual is unique, every situation has its own set of variables. We can't expect to unravel the mechanics of mankind's emotional landscape, we're just looking for clues, for signs along the road. If we have some level of understanding of an individual's needs and preferences, we can make some pretty safe assumptions about what will translate and where it might break down. If we can anticipate how someone may react under pressure, perhaps we can neutralize the stress before it occurs.

My goal is to bring awareness, to start the conversation. The old saying, "If the shoe fits, wear it," applies. If you think you may be a *Controller*, try to be more self-aware and regulate accordingly. If you are bridge building to span the chasm between you and a *Controller*, be it your boss, a coworker or your child, leverage your new perspectives.

Clichés lack creativity but they contain truth. "Stress brings out the worst in us." is one that comes to mind. We are human beings, don't be surprised when the worst in you surfaces. The faster we recognize the negative impact of our behavior under stress, the faster we can recover.

Don't take things personally when you're dealing with people in stressful situations. Don't be surprised once that memo goes to the Autonomic Nervous System and you find you're in *fight or flight*. If your team is struggling, and you come in on Monday morning, step into your *Controller*-designed manager's office and begin with, "Hey Linda, how was your weekend? Can you believe the weather we're having?" Well, that might feel good to you, but what might feel good to your *Controller* manager is something like, "Hi Linda, here's the report on activity you asked for, I worked on it over the weekend. I have some ideas to discuss when you have time."

If you are a *Controller* design, and someone walks into your office Monday morning when you are behind the eight-ball and wants to talk about how bad the Lakers are this year, take a breath, then take another one. Understand they don't feel urgency and the drive for results like you do. Just say, "Yeah, they're lost right now, can you get me the activity reports from last weekend?"

Rock Your Gig takes self-awareness, an understanding of others' needs and a willingness to alter your approach. We will discuss Versatility in upcoming pages. For now, let's move on and meet **The Creator**.

THE CREATOR SEES THE BIG PICTURE,
HAS THE BIG IDEAS
AND THE SKILLS
TO BRING OTHERS ALONG.

CHAPTER 9

THE CREATOR

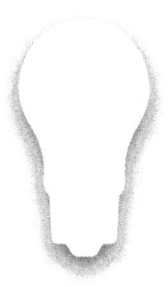

THE CREATOR

DEFINING BEHAVIORAL CHARACTERISTICS

The *Creator* lights it up! They have ideas, lots of them, and they can't wait to share them with you, or really anyone that's interested! Like the *Controller*, their Tell-Assertive orientation reflects confidence and commitment. Unlike Controllers, the *Creator* design is more people responsive, and they share their emotions more freely, sometimes to a fault. The *Creator* works from a foundation of feelings, "I feel, therefor…" versus, "I know", "I think" or "I like". *Creators* are just as interested in how you feel and want to hear and support your ideas. Their responsiveness translates as passion, their assertiveness as energy. Vision, passion and energy are just a few of the strengths of the *Creator* design.

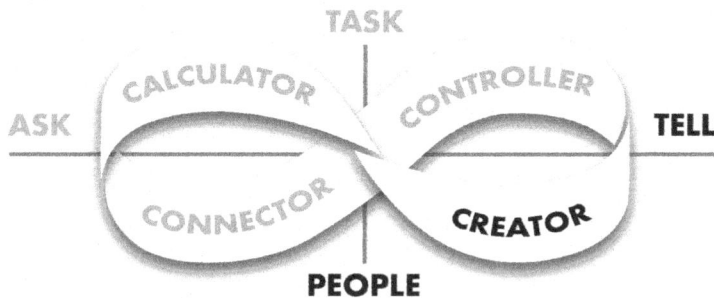

9a. The Creator: TELL-assertive, PEOPLE-oriented

I'm a *Creator*. That's right, an idea-man, like Michael Keaton in *Night Shift*, "*Wait, wait…what if we take live tuna fish, and feed them mayonnaise! This is gonna be huge, we'll call it Startkist."* Well, maybe a slightly more self-edited version, but you get my drift. Lots of ideas being sold with lots of passion. One of the biggest lessons I learned about my *Creator* design was just that, passion. My time at Fender, through the lens of my *Creator* design, helped me form this perspective.

Here's a quick sidebar for you *Creators* out there. (*Controllers*, I know your bored, breathe, exhale longer than you inhale…4 in, 6 out, good.) I was asked to participate in an executive development program at Fender. I wasn't asked if I *wanted* to participate, I was asked to participate. It pretty much felt like non-elective corporate counseling to me, because it was. I was a Senior Vice President and our executive team was pretty dysfunctional. The economy was in a steep recession and we were under a ton of pressure to keep the business financially balanced and moving forward. We didn't understand each other and our critical thinking eroded into ugly debate, it felt like it was an election year, every year. Respect was on a wanted poster but nowhere to be found. Make no mistake, everyone at Fender loves and honors the brand, everyone I ever worked with was always defending a position out of a true belief they were doing what was best for the brand, including me.

I don't want to minimize this, but I do want to move on, so I'll summarize quickly. The program was amazing. I was privileged to worked with a seasoned mentor for six months. By the conclusion of the program, he had injected a big dose of objective self-awareness into my psyche. It triggered *The Spirit of Reinvention* at a critical intersection in my life and positively influenced my career and relationships at home. It also made me weep.

One of the facets of the program was, of course, the 360° review. This was a little more comprehensive than a standard review, it went in every direction; over, under, sideways down. It was a really sophisticated assessment, so I'll summarize: "Richard is a creative, charismatic, inspirational …ass!" Oh man, that was hard for me to hear. I was told, "Richard, your passion isn't a license to be an a-hole when things don't go the way you want them to."

Creators, this is a trap you can fall into occasionally. If you are working with, in love with, or raising a *Creator*, expect a ride on the roller coaster of emotions every now and then. We will discuss navigational tips for *Creators* in the upcoming chapters.

Our greatest strength can be our greatest weakness if we don't have a purposeful approach, focus and the ability to regulate.

• **The Creator** is a powerful motivator with vision and energy. Their enthusiasm can be infectious.

• **The Creator** loves to trade "chops" aka exchange ideas. They are genuinely interested in your ideas and how you feel about them.

• **The Creator** is a little disorganized, or even really disorganized. Their responsiveness is emotionally, not task, oriented. Ok, come on in, find a seat, "sorry, sorry I'm late, no problemo..." I was just saying the *Creator* can be a little disorganized.

• **The Creator** sees the big picture, has big ideas and the skills to bring others along. Somebody has to be the first one to suggest streaking, to be the first to take their clothes off and convince others to follow suit(less.)

• **The Creator** wants to be seen as a unique and creative thought leader. Their work style is to motivate the team and reinforce the vision.

• **The Creator** typically thinks fast and speaks fast. They use their voice for inflection and emphasis. The more excited they get, the faster and louder they get.

• **The Creator** is assertively expressive and frequently uses bold, non-verbal forms of communication; hand gestures, emotive eyes, smiles and frowns.

• **The Creator** likes to work on teams, sharing and elevating ideas. Their "tell" orientation is balanced by their responsiveness—they brake for small animals.

- **The Creator** is motivated by recognition, visibility and respect. To accomplish this, they are comfortable in the spotlight—*really* comfortable in the spotlight, as a matter of fact, "Can you bring the band down behind me a little? Thanks."

- **The Creator** can be original in their attire, utilizing it to demonstrate their creativity and uniqueness. Their originality is part of their identity.

Does this sound like anyone you know? Write their names in your journal and let's take a look at the *Creator* under stress.

CREATOR DESIGN UNDER STRESS

We discussed some of the nuances of Personality Designs Under Stress in the *Controller* focused segment, so let's move right into the behavioral characteristics of Creators when things get sticky. The *Take It To The Bridge* chapter will bring all these observations into practical application. Keep reading!

- **The Creator** is Tell Assertive. Their orientation in stressful situations is *fight*. They can be quick to attack.

- **The Creator** under tension will rely on their strengths, leveraging emotions and feelings, but with a negative aggressive tone.

- **The Creator** typically inspires and creates esteem in others, but under stress they can become accusatory and make others feel at fault.

- **The Creator** under pressure *sells* even harder. Their tendency to brush over the details can create confusion, the more questions they can't answer the more they sell.

- **The Creator** can be quick tempered. Your position in their eyes can change rapidly. All of a sudden, all *your* great ideas are whimsical and not taken seriously (and neither are you).

- **The Creator** may shutdown if the disfunction passes a point. They're just temporarily out of ideas. Their responsiveness pushes them toward people. They want positive connectivity with others. They will wipe the board clean and start again. Ultimately, they believe in "people power."

THEY HAVE THE CAPACITY
TO LISTEN, NOT JUST HEAR.
THEY LISTEN INTENTLY AND
UNDERSTAND DEEPLY.

CHAPTER 10

THE CONNECTOR

CHAPTER 10.

THE CONNECTOR

DEFINING BEHAVIORAL CHARACTERISTICS
THE CONECTOR

The *Connector* is everyone's BFF. The *Connector* lives at the corner of People Street and Hugs Avenue. Their calm, open demeanor just screams, "Come in have a good cry, tell me all about it." They're like your personal psychiatrist, (you just don't have to talk about your mother.) They have the capacity to listen, not just hear. They listen intently and understand deeply. They get matters of the heart and possess a high level of emotional intelligence. You and your secrets are safe with them. Kind and compassionate, leading with their emotional instinct and a desire to serve, they always want to be part of the team. How nice the world would be if each one of us were a calm, cool, *Connector*.

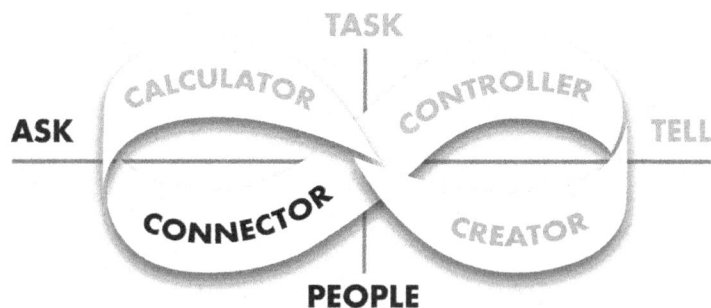

10a. The Connector: ASK-assertive, PEOPLE-oriented

It would be amazingly nice, and we would never, ever, get anything done! On the other hand, we wouldn't even care if we didn't get anything done, as long as we enjoyed our time together.

My son Micah is a *Connector*, my wife Lisa is a hybrid *Connector*, my sister Phyllis is a *Connector*, my buddy Gene is a *Connector*. These are the people I am closest to, and from an assertiveness perspective, the least like. I'm loud, they're not. I like the spotlight, they don't. My friends and family are much better at being friends and family, than I am. The *Connector* "gets it."

Don't get me wrong, they're not all fluff-and-no-stuff Winnie the Pooh types. Remember these are organic personality behaviors. Successful individuals are self-aware and able to purposefully enhance or alter their approach. They surround themselves with people that enhance their personality design and broadened their appeal. Our thirty-ninth and fortieth presidents (Jimmy Carter and Ronald Reagan), were both *Connector*, "people first" people. Even though one was a Democrat (Carter) and one a Republican (Regan). Former First Lady, Michelle Obama is a shining example of a strong, inspirational *Connector*.

I have observed the *Connector's* "Relationship First" policy at play in the global business arena as well. Up front, the traditional Japanese business culture is all about the relationship. Trust and credibility have to be established as a priority. I recall my first excursions to Asia, and specifically Japan, wondering if we were ever going to get down to business. You know, commerce, "Let's get a deal, put some ink on paper." Slow down John Wayne. Eventually, we would get deep into the details (with massive hangovers and raw karaoke-nicotine-throat), I would come home with—ta da! No orders. Two weeks later they would come rattling off of the fax machine. Similarly, *Connectors* need to know who they are dealing with and feel safe before they commit, and that can take time.

• **The Connector** is the friend that actually gives you good advice. They are great active listeners and create comfort.

• **The Connector** has a careful cadence when they speak. They are often soft spoken. They can sometimes have a hard time breaking through in assertive group environments.

- **The Connector** will take the initiative in establishing new relationships. If you sit down next to a *Connector* on a flight, expect to meet them, learn where they work, share where you work, where you are going and why. Today is the best day to make a new friend.

- **The Connector** has an open, inviting nonverbal posture. They're warm and receptive vibe is visible.

- **The Connector** prefers coaching roles and encouraging teams versus being on the field themselves. They're satisfaction is through involvement with others, being part of the team.

- **The Connector** wants to have a positive impact on others, to assist and serve.

- **The Connector** might sing, "everything is awesome, everything is awesome, when you're part of a team." Yes, Emmit the Lego[22] is a *Connector* too.

- **The Connector**, true to their design, is the connective tissue on many teams. There Ask-Responsive design restores calm, breaks down walls and brings people together.

- **The Connector** is patient and has a calm, mature demeanor.

- **The Connector** is energized by the team dynamic, they never miss a pep rally, town hall, Spirit Week or class reunion. In fact, there is no class reunion without the *Connector*.

- **The Connector** will tend to navigate away from conflict.

- **The Connector** is likely the person that will come by your desk when you're busy as heck and want to chat. Unlike other designs they don't feel or like, urgency.

- **The Connector** accepts others individuality and wants to see people getting along together.

- **The Connector** is easy to get to know, their open style welcomes relationships.

- **The Connector** can defuse a situation through independent diplomacy. They are always a willing people-partner.

- **The Connector** will always help you move. I, on the other hand, will probably come up with as many excuses as needed to get out of your moving adventure.

- **The Connector** works from a foundation of "I like, therefor..." versus "I think, I know or I feel."

At this point, you should have a list of friends, family and acquaintances fitting the *Connector* personality design. Let's move on to stress behaviors and triggers of the *Connector*.

THE CONNECTOR DESIGN UNDER STRESS

As calm as the *Connector* appears on the surface, their Ask-Assertive design, combined with higher emotional responsiveness can make them vulnerable to stress when assertive people are being, you know, assertive people.

Their brain's autonomic division has its finger on the *flight* button, ready to sound the sympathetic chemical alarm at the first sign of friction. The *Connector* doesn't like conflict, they avoid it at all costs. Their default mitigation plan is to acquiesce. Don't expect a robust debate with the *Connector*, it will be a short one.

- **The Connector** can take criticism personally. When they do, they tend to shut down versus debate. Even if they are right.

- **The Connector** may not be completely forthcoming with information if they believe it may create conflict.

- **The Connector** does not respond to pushing and prodding. It stresses them out and further erodes their productivity. They are not Task-oriented, it's not the first thing they think about. They need to feel safe first.

- **The Connector** can be put out of sync with you because of a faltering relationship you have with someone else. They feel and share others stress as well as their own. The *Connector* designs in my life are always there to let me know when I've stepped on someone's emotional toe (if I wrestle it out of them!) "What's up? You have a big smudge in your aura? I did what? Oh man, I'll call him and make sure everything is cool."

• **The Connector** is emotionally rich much like the *Creator*, but their Ask Assertiveness triggers *flight*, in contrast to the willingness to jump in the ring *fight* of the *Creator*.

• **The Connector's** nonverbal demeanor is typically open, though their inviting body language can close down under stress. Sulking is always an option.

• **The Connector** can be stubborn and rigid under stress. Doing things out of spite isn't out of the question.

• **The Connector** owns a helpful nature that can lead to over commitment, followed by stress and frustration. Deadlines, or too many things on their plate at once can cause them to shut down.

• **The Connector** willl never get it done fast enough.

We will discuss approaches and ideas for neutralizing stress with the *Connector* in the upcoming *Take it to the Bridge* chapter. Stay tuned, especially you *Controller* types!

If you are a *Connector*, thank you for being you! We are lost without you. Look back at your Objective Self-Assessment SWOT. There might be opportunities to take on a little more responsibility, be a little more organized and accountable. Find someone with whom you feel safe and practice giving them direct feedback.

If you are a *Controller.* Don't run over the *Connector.* Respect what they bring to the team. Slow down, don't have an agenda for once, just be relaxed, engage. Don't push them, inspire them!

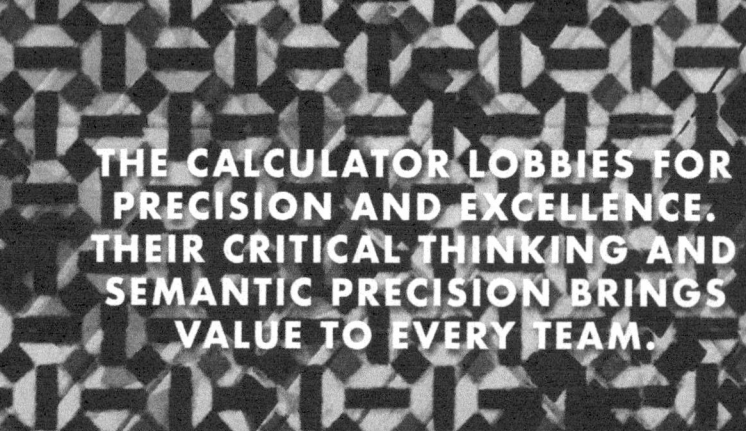

THE CALCULATOR LOBBIES FOR
PRECISION AND EXCELLENCE.
THEIR CRITICAL THINKING AND
SEMANTIC PRECISION BRINGS
VALUE TO EVERY TEAM.

CHAPTER 11

THE CALCULATOR

CHAPTER 11.

THE CALCULATOR

DEFINING BEHAVIORAL CHARACTERISTICS

When I first made the transition from musician to company guy, data types were in a department called M.I.S. or Management Information Systems. It was behind a locked door with a push button combination. There weren't retinal scanners at the time, or they would have had them. The M.I.S. agents would look over their shoulder, skylark left and right, and pull in close as they punched the code. Another quick look around, the door would open just enough to slide through, and with a whisk and click they were gone. A mystery wrapped in an enigma. Didn't even say goodbye.

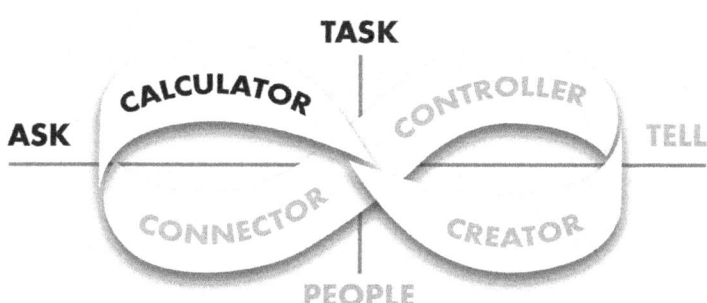

11a. The Calculator: ASK-assertive, TASK-oriented

The team in M.I.S. at the time was best described as, "birds of a feather that calculated together." I had yet to realize that a personality design occasionally worked and nested together in a community. It was like a club for quiet, thoughtful people with serious attention spans. There was another group of *Calculator* types comfortably nesting in the Engineering department as well. There was plenty of diversity, and there was a common thread of capability that ran through them all. They were a systems-oriented team, not a people-oriented team. It was like being in a band with all keyboard players. They were precise and had an appetite for every nuance of their playing—and yours! "Did you mean to play that?""What are you talking about? I was having a moment …ok? "Ya, I was just wondering, if you meant to play that…"

• **The Calculator** possess strong analytical skills. They can do the math. The sciences, IT, Engineering, Finance are all career disciplines where the Calculator may leverage their personality design strengths.

• **The Calculator** has the capacity to untie knots that you and I just stare at. They think a Rubik's Cube is fun. It's not that they can write code, it's that they *like* to write code.

• **The Calculator** has a slow, steady cadence to their deliberate, articulate, speech. They come across relaxed and thoughtful.

• **The Calculator** doesn't rely on bold nonverbal gestures or voice inflection for emphasis, and they don't understand why you do.

• **The Calculator** won't be the one to break the ice in a new relationship. Which is awesome if your flight is late, your exhausted and don't feel like talking, sit next to a *Calculator* and don't make eye contact, get some rest.

• **The Calculator** operates from a position of "I think therefor..." versus "I like, I feel or I know."They need to be right, to have done the work, to know they are right, the perspective is correct. Your timeline? Not so much.

• **The Calculator** will say things like, "We never have time to do it right, but we have time to do it over, and over again." They may be right, or they may be in a whirlpool of indecision.

• **The Calculator** invented "analysis paralysis." Just when you think you're there they say, "Let's add a column."

• **The Calculator** likes to consider all the potential before starting something new. This includes relationships. Mid-stream course changes can be frustrating for them.

• **The Calculator** can be critical and appear emotionally detached. Their Task orientation responsiveness can be isolating.

• **The Calculator** is there when it absolutely, positively has to be right. Triple-checked and pressure tested with a parallel system running for backup.

• **The Calculator** doesn't like to be pushed. "Do you want it now, or do you want it right?"

• **The Calculator** likes defining process. Sometimes, it appears like they are more enthused by the process then the outcome.

• **The Calculator** can be more formal and conservative in attire and demeanor. They own a sense of appropriateness.

• **The Calculator** has a strong work ethic and takes a measured, systematic approach to everything. Improvisational solutions make them very uneasy.

• **The Calculator** lobbies for precision and excellence. Their critical thinking and semantic precision brings value to every team. Their Task Responsive orientation can make them a little harder to get to know, but they're in there, take your time.

The details don't get past the *Calculator*, their processes and protocol assure it. The occasional, "can't see the forest for the trees" moment should be anticipated. Give them the brain games and turn them loose.

Ok, I know that you know a few *Calculator* types. Take a minute and write down their names. If there is a specific interpersonal challenge you are having with a *Calculator*, all the better. We are looking for opportunities to make positive connections. We will discuss approaches to take with *Calculators,* as well as all 4C Designs in the chapters ahead. First, let's examine *Calculators* under Pressure.

THE CALCULATOR DESIGN UNDER STRESS

"Open the pod-bay door HAL. Hello, HAL, do you read me?"

"Affirmative Dave, I read you."

"Open the pod-bay doors Hal."

"I'm sorry Dave, I'm afraid I can't do that."

"What's the problem?"

"I think you know what the problem is, just as well as I do."

'What are you talking about HAL?"

"This mission is too important for me to allow you to jeopardize it."

– 2001 A Space Odyssey[23]

• **The Calculator** under pressure can be challenging. You may feel like Dave, trying to get back into the pod-bay. Once it reaches a tipping point, the *Calculator* will shift into *flight* mode and shut down.

Their go-to behavior in stressful situations will be avoidance. You have been rescheduled, I just didn't have time to call you back, return your email or text.

• **The Calculator** can be highly critical and close off physically in stressful situation. Arms crossed, no eye contact, even fewer words.

These are the bold defining behaviors of a personality design under stress. Remember, it's on a continuum. There are *Calculator* types on the cusp of being a *Connector* with a higher degree of responsiveness. You know, the chatty math teacher that coaches volleyball. And people drop to the east on the Assertiveness scale toward a Tell Assertive orientation as well. The objective isn't to hit a personality design bullseye, it's to give you a clue where to look and what to do when you get there. It's directional. Be yourself but have an elevated awareness of others' needs and preferences. It may get you back through the pod-bay doors.

VERSATILITY IS DEFINED
AS OUR ABILITY TO ADAPT
TO MANY DIFFERENT FUNCTIONS
OR ACTIVITIES.

RYG:
METHODS
AND
TOOLS

CHAPTER 12.

ROCKING the GIG: METHODS and TOOLS

We are building a foundational belief system. The power of the *Rock Your Gig* philosophy is in the compounding and interplay of these perspectives. The whole being greater than the sum of its parts. It's important to sustain a wholistic view. To that end, let's review what we have established before we roll up our sleeves and take on the final pieces of the puzzle.

THE ROCK YOUR GIG PHILOSOPHY

• **We believe in the *Spirit of Reinvention*.**

We understand the opportunity to reimagine our lives is powerful and is ours for the taking if we have the motivation and courage.

• **Objective self-awareness is essential.**

Understanding our *Strengths, Weaknesses, Opportunities* and *Threats* (SWOT) defines our *Field of Opportunity*.

• **We are functioning in an integrated and interdependent environment we refer to as the Ecosystem of You.**

The health status of the ecosystem is positively and negatively affected by our physical, emotional and spiritual health.

• **The first step in restructuring a suffering ecosystem is to snap out of the illusions of the status quo.**

Keanu Reeves' made an unimaginably bold observation in a fun movie, *"We are all asleep, living in a destructive yet comfortable illusion."*

• **The best process for evaluating the status of our personal** ecosystem is to survey and seek a higher level of life balance. *Rock Your Gig* takes an Integrated perspective on life balance.

• **The 4C Personality design matrix gives us a framework, a point of reflection to create elevated understanding of the needs and preferences of others.**

• **We know this; as unlikely as it seems, the path to abundance is paved by meeting the needs of others first.**

• **We can get a quick read by asking ourselves two questions:**

1. How Assertive? 2. How Emotional?

• **Plot the axes to reveal the personality design.**

• **We know the way people behave interpersonally is not a reflection of how they truly feel.**

• **We know everyone has emotions.**

The *Controller* and the *Calculator* have the same emotions as the *Connector* and the *Creator*—they just don't expose or share them as easily.

• **We know each personality design is perfect, and capable of anything.**

It's in our design. If we are an east of the meridian *Controller* or *Creator* we are likely to *fight*. West of the meridian, *flight* is the sympathetic nervous system's preference of the *Calculator* and the *Connector*.

• **We understand we shouldn't overthink this.**

It's not the reason people do things. It doesn't answer the question, "Why." It's an observation we can make about the needs and preferences of others.

Ok, let's move to the next phase. Effective communication across the *4C Personality Designs*.

Effective Communication

Creating positive connectivity requires effective communication. This is another area where we are typically on autopilot. We have to "be" or we would never get anything done. Like many of our default responses, automatic responses are one-size-fits-all at best. Probably more accurate to one's size, the one that fits "me."

Who could imagine walking through life and pausing before every interpersonal encounter to consider a purposeful approach? I'm not recommending that, it sounds weird and wrong to begin with. I can whole-heartedly endorse trying to do it when it really matters. Don't use your standard, "They get me." approach with someone under stress. Like I did.

I arrived at London's Gatwick Airport after a long night of flying. It was my first business trip to Europe. Trying to get my bearings and feeling somewhere between Austin Powers: International Man of Mystery and Han Solo at the edge of the galaxy, I turned and rather clumsily and bumped right into Princess Leia! "Excuse me." I offered with an apologetic look on my face. "Excuse me? You run into me!" she stingingly offered with a rich cockney accent that made it even more penetrating. She went on, "Excuse me my ass, I've a mind to run me gums upside your head!" She walked away mumbling a stream of insults.

I was dumbfounded. I saw my associate and host across the terminal and walked his way. I explained what happened, he listened and laughed so hard I thought I wet his pants. "Richard," he offered, "We are English we say we're 'Sorry', even when we don't mean it!" Excuse me translated as, "You owe me an apology." Oh man, I felt so dumb. Two countries separated by a common language. Now it was making sense. I think I bought the book *Kiss, Bow or Shake Hands*[24] when I got back to the states. I realized I needed to understand international business culture a lot better.

Guess what? The translation can get just as jacked-up with someone at home or at work. You don't have to travel halfway around the world to experience misconnection, you can have that fun right outside your door. We have the opportunity to elevate the effectiveness of our communication and add energy and clarity to our transmissions. My "cockney collision" was a huge moment of learning for me. When you run into a communication conundrum, make sure you learn from it too.

A UCLA study performed by Albert Mehrabian[25] determined the effectiveness of communication is based on three key factors:

1. The words we choose.
2. The way we say them, our tone.
3. The associated nonverbal color.

As a man of many words (contrary to my UK airport experience), I was shocked to learn that about 7% of the effectiveness of our communication is the script. "Wait...what...really?" Yes. Think about it. Take the word, "Thanks." It can be a sincere form of gratitude or a stinging jab depending on the tone and body language accompanying it.

A third of the effectiveness is generated by the tone and volume of our transmissions. You can be 100% right and it doesn't mean a thing if your tone blocks the transmission.

Here is where the brain-blow occurs: over half of the effectiveness of our communication is nonverbal facial expressions and body language. No wonder email is such a poor interpersonal medium! And so, emojis came to be. So, the next time someone is trying to explain something to you, and you are across the room with your arms crossed in front of you, put your hands in your pockets and take a step forward. Put your defenses down and give them a chance.

Before we enter into any dynamic interpersonal environment, we want to tune and align our nonverbal posture to increase the effectiveness of our communication. This is, of course, dependent of the personality design with whom we are involved. Let' take a closer look.

NONVERBAL COMMUNICATION

Once again, let's start with *where to look*. Nonverbal communication spans a wide range, lets focus on a few, beginning with...

• Facial Expressions

Our faces are capable of expressing the full gamut of human emotion. We can see it today in animated films, artists are able to reflect the full human emotional spectrum on a robot shaped like an egg, with two glowing orbs for eyes. Its absolutely amazing. The symphony of our subtle inflections in the eyes and the mouths are especially expressive. You don't need to be a sage to see fear, anxiety, sadness, happiness, confusion, anger or disgust. You just need to be looking for the signs, to be interested in their emotional state, comfort and safety.

• Rapid Blinking of Eyes

This can be a sign of stress and discomfort. Eyes artificially held still may be a sign someone is trying to control their emotions, think "poker face."

• Rolling Eyes

Disbelief with a dash of contempt. You have a credibility issue

• Dilated Pupils

This can be a sign of fear or excitement! The situation will dictate whether they are afraid or in love ...or on drugs.

• Tightly Pursed Lips

This could be a sign of disapproval or possibly a lack of trust. Biting lips nervously usually means stressed or worried. The edge of the mouth turning down unhappy, up at the edges means happy. Unless they have recently been to the dentist, then ignore all mouth related cues.

• Arm Signals

Crossed in front is a defensive posture. Arms on your hips is a power pose and can be interpreted as threatening in some situations. Arms behind your back is a sign of confidence and contemplation, or they can be bored and pissed off. We need to look at it holistically. Face, tone, body, position. You'll know if they have a smudge in their aura, the mystery will be, "Why?"

• Rapid Tapping of the Fingers

Can signal boredom or frustration, or you may be dealing with a drummer (they just can't stop.) Kinetic learners will tend to fidget, that's why they invented fidget-spinners.

• Leg Signals

Our legs tell a story as well. Closed posture can be a sign of discomfort or anxiety or it can mean you're wearing a dress, thank you. Open legs, inviting and friendly.

• Touching the Face

Playing with hair, mouth, eyes or ears can be a sign of discomfort and concern.

Again, I really believe the secret is in caring enough to look for the signs. Actively survey, don't just stare through people. Look at them and into them.

On the other side of the table. Consider what posture and nonverbal expressions you are bringing into your interpersonal moments. Are you an aggressive *Creator* who leans forward in the chair, eyes wide with excitement? In some situations, you can actually scare the heck out of people.

The remaining 30% of our effectiveness, is our tone. If you are a *Creator* or *Controller*, like me, then know that your tongue and the public address system behind it is so powerful it can potentially move mountains–and every now and then, we move them right on top of other people.

Be accountable for what comes out of your mouth. It can inspire or demotivate depending on how you say what you say. Less assertive personality designs, specifically those on the west side of the assertiveness line, can be short circuited by the pace, tone and inflection of your communication. If you are raising kids this is crucial. Your verbal tone and approach can undermine their self-esteem. They don't understand it's not what you truly feel. As a matter of fact, most people won't put that together. They will take your tone and approach personally. And if they don't like it, they are unlikely to be your champion. Remember, your goal is to get promoted!

We should have an elevated perspective on communication at this point. Our tone and approach matter a lot and our nonverbal accompaniment is king. We move forward with increased awareness and sensitivity to how we come across and how to get a read on others.

Our body language sets the table for positive connectivity. Our tone and approach create a safe environment for openness and assures our message will be heard.

We can add this to our compounded perspective and move forward. By understanding what effective communication actually looks like we can take a more purposeful approach to our interpersonal encounters. Anyone in sales (and by the way, we are all in sales), should tune in closely. Tough accounts are great places to hone your interpersonal chops. Or perhaps your spouse or child is your toughest account. It works there too.

AUTO-RESPONSE TO OTHERS BEHAVIOR

Here are three automated functions to which we rarely give a second thought. How do we decide what our behavioral reactions are going to be? Ha, we don't!

1. Witness

What we observe or experience in others behavior. All our senses at work as we systematically process, organize and focus on the event. It all occurs in milli-seconds.

2. Conclude

Based on a whole bunch of stuff, like our beliefs, our experiences, context and personal bias, we arrive at a conclusion. "She doesn't like me." "He's mad" "I'm glad that's not me." It's neatly packaged in a box and it didn't even take a second.

3. Reaction

Can you say, "AUTOMATIC?" Default behavioral response activated and engaged. Just like that. It is completely reactive. I'll say it again, It's totally reactive. The ball comes over the net, we hit it back, or walk away. There is another way to *Rock Yout Gig.*

PURPOSEFUL VERSATILITY

This is where we put it all together and put it to work. Up to this point, it's been about preparation. Preparing ourselves to take a new path. We have invited the Spirit of Reinvention into our lives and assumed the mantle of elevated Self-Awareness. We have new insights and tools to sustain health and balance in our personal ecosystem. We can now recognize the 4C Personality Designs by their dominate behaviors and we understand our automated behavioral reactions that don't help our cause. I think we are ready. Let's start by taking our behavioral reactions out of AUTOMATIC and flip the switch to MANUAL MODE. Let's take the wheel.

What do I mean by "purposeful versatility?" Break it down. Purposeful meaning "on purpose", that one is pretty clear. Purposeful or intentional in nature, not default or random. Versatility is defined as our ability to adapt to many different functions or activities. This is where we need to make some adjustments.

We are focused on interpersonal versatility, defined as our ability to create positive connectivity outside our personality design. Now we need to add the flexibility to step outside of what we need to consider the needs of *others*, and consider them with purpose.

We should stop here for a moment. I am not saying, "Step outside the comfort of your design and pretend to be someone else!" No. Not in any way, shape or form should you ever do that! Why would you abandon your perfect design in the first place? You're too cool just the way you are. It's way more subtle and honoring than that. It can be as simple as slowing down your speech or speeding it up to create comfort. It's offering a house guest a glass of water and an appropriate place to sit. Not any place to sit, an *appropriate* place to sit. It's being considerate, not Machiavellian.

If you still feel like I am asking you to abandon your cool, complicated, brooding vibe, it's because I am–for a minute. If it's not serving you and you're making others uncomfortable (and by doing so not getting what you need either), take your emotional hoodie off and smile!

Like our automatic behavioral responses, purposeful versatility has three specific stages; Identify, Visualize and Customize. Unlike our automated reactionary process, Applied Versatility is purposeful and proactive.

• Identify the Design

Our automatic response system reacts quickly, that's why our species is still around! The idea is to quickly stop "passive observation" and kick in "active identification". Where do they fall on the Personality Design Möbius? Don't over think this. If it's someone you know it should be easy. Think assertiveness first, it's always easy to see and equally conspicuous in its absence.

Divide the möbius in half. North or South, Task or People? Speech, fast and abbreviated or thoughtful and deliberate? Do this in a second or two, not milli-seconds. Yes, slow down. It doesn't need to be as fast as your automatic reaction. Stop and process, focus on identifying the design.

• Visualize the Need

Are they showing signs of stress? Are they joyful? What is their body language telling you? Visualize what will close the gap, take the pressure off them a bit, let you get a little closer, and lay down a smooth, positive groove. Try to see their need. Your automated approach may have told you this is a one act play, perhaps it should be two or three acts.

Visualizing needs isn't always about unraveling a problem! Meeting and exceeding the needs of others includes supporting behaviors, inspiring behaviors and honoring behaviors. Understanding their personality design allows us to choose an approach that will optimize positive connectivity.

• Customize Your Approach

This is it, the moment of truth. Phase three is where we stop thinking and step into the interpersonal arena! If that metaphor conjures visions of gladiators doing battle, then let's adjust. Stop thinking and confidently stroll onto the interpersonal dance floor. Either way, let's get busy. Everything we have discussed to this point is about to manifest itself in your social behavior. The stage is set, lights fade, and you are on!

Your demeanor is a reflection of the state of your personal ecosystem and your cognitive perspective (aka mood). It all comes together to construct the "you" others perceive. Remember, nonverbal cues are a dominate factor in the overall effectiveness of communication. Is your transmission weak and fuzzy, or strong and clear?

We have to see ourselves first, be self-aware, know who we are bringing through the door. Is it an energized and focused posture, or something less? I can recall being in an intense meeting at the end of the day that left me with a lot of frustrated, dark energy. We only lived a short distance from the office at the time, and when I brought all that emotional baggage through the door, Lisa astutely remarked, "Maybe you should take the long way home."

Before we ever say a word, we will speak volumes.

You may feel like Neil Armstrong taking that first "small step for man" when you leave the comfort and safety of your design for the first time. Know this customized approach is what elevates and sustains healthy relationships. This is bridge building, extending beyond the comfort of our shores, to create safe passage for others. Extending beyond your design takes versatility.

Versatility and a strong sense of self go hand-in-hand. You have to be self-confident to set your needs and preferences aside and consider those of others. We can tell ourselves we are selling out, or giving into "the man", and not being true to ourselves. But being an interpersonally versatile person isn't selling out, it's stepping up!

Be versatile and flexible in your approach to others. Universal approaches do not work. Be mindful and make small adjustments to your design's default behaviors to accommodate the situational need. It's not an academy award performance. We are looking for the sincere, authentic and thoughtful "you." You can stand firm and take every wave in the face, or you can learn to surf. Versatility reduces the need for resilience

Each personality design has specific situational needs. Some are even shared by two or more designs. To bring the complete *Rock Your Gig* philosophy to life, we need two final perspectives. **In any given interpersonal situation, remember these two things:**

1. **What needs and preferences do I observe in another's personality design?**

2. **What adjustments do I need to make to my default behaviors given my personality design?**

Let's dig-in and see what this looks like in each of the 4Cs, from both sides of the situational table. We have a pretty good idea what the bold behaviors look like. If we have done our homework, we have examples to use as icons from familiar family, friends, and coworkers. **It's time to take it to the bridge!**

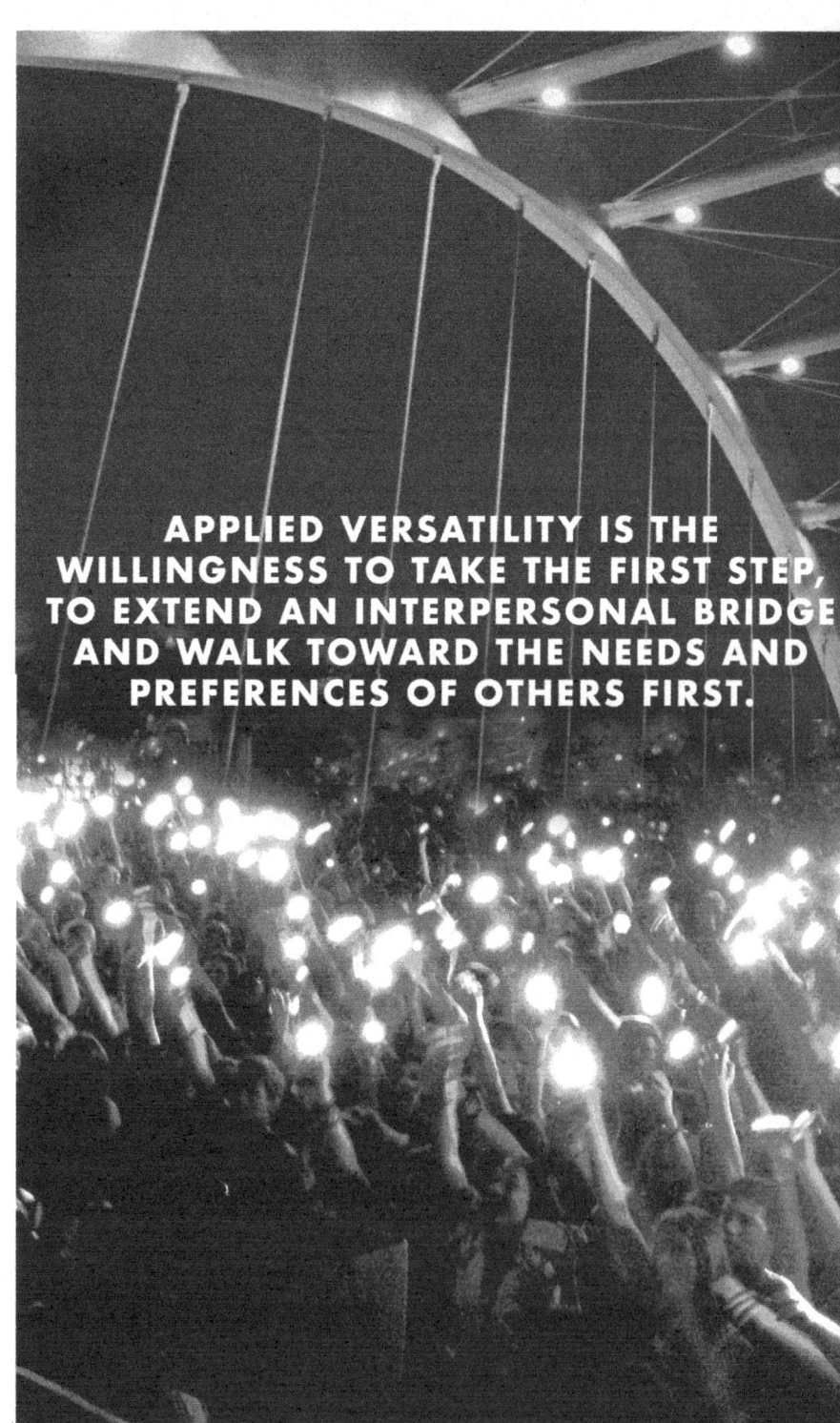

APPLIED VERSATILITY IS THE WILLINGNESS TO TAKE THE FIRST STEP, TO EXTEND AN INTERPERSONAL BRIDGE AND WALK TOWARD THE NEEDS AND PREFERENCES OF OTHERS FIRST.

CHAPTER 13

TAKE IT
TO THE
BRIDGE

CHAPTER 13.

BRIDGE BUILDING 101

The *Rock Your Gig* philosophy, as you know, borrows from the business playbook. This process-and-plan approach gives form and dimension to misty topics like self-awareness, balance and optimizing interpersonal effectiveness. We need an approach we can later evaluate and refine, not a moving target of variables. An approach born by a set of beliefs, versus randomness and automatic default behaviors.

It's easy, in the midst of a busy day with a packed calendar, to merely *show up* to an interpersonal moment. It's just another meeting in a long, blurry succession of meetings. When we turn off and tune out, we miss opportunities for positive connectivity; the moments that expand the *Field of Opportunity* in our lives. We want to rise above the status quo, positively differentiate ourselves, elevate the importance of every encounter and treat them all with purpose and respect.

Let's adopt an engagement protocol for every meaningful encounter. Here is a format that never disappoints. It's pretty simple, we know it as: the *Beginning,* the *Middle* and the *End.* A business operations type might say Preparation, Execution and Review. The Category Merchant is thinking *Before, During* and *After* the sale. It's intentional and repeatable. This perspective is for more formal, face to face interactions, but we can use it effectively at home with our children as well. Everyone values respect and clarity. Please read on for the *Rock Your Gig* three-step interpersonal approach.

THREE STAGES of INTERPERSONAL ENGAGEMENT

In any given interpersonal situation:

- What needs and preferences do I observe in another's personality design?
- What adjustments do I need to make to my default behaviors given my personality design?

If we know who we are dealing with we would skip the design assessment phase and go right to customization. However, if we are engaged with someone new, we may need to make a quick assessment, a rough cut to help identify this new encounter's personality design.

1. Getting into the moment—gracefully

The goal is to establish trust, comfort and credibility as early as possible. We start by understand the needs and preferences of the personality design we are working with. More to follow here.

2. Having the moment—effectively

The goal is to develop a common base of understanding of the issue at hand. Start by uncovering, soliciting their perspective first. Use active listening, nonverbal acknowledgments and note taking. Once again, understanding their personality design will dictate the pace and subject matter of the conversation. .

3. Closing the moment—with clarity

The goal is alignment. Affirm and restate any agreements. Not all conversations end in agreement, but you need clarity at all costs. Don't miss opportunities to set up the next moment of positive connectivity. In Sales situations, for example, there are opportunities for meaningful engagement that come from commonality and understanding needs.

We have our process outlined so we won't take a free-form jazz odyssey approach and improvise our way through. I personally used this approach too long (and though I love *Spinal Tap*, I don't even like jazz.) Now we have to color it in. Let's repeat, our primary objective is to determine two things...

Personality Design Quick Assessment

I had the privilege of serving in the United States Coast Guard. I was trained as a Sonar Systems Technician at the Naval Training Center in San Diego, Ca. I was part of a small team of electronic technicians that operated, serviced and repaired the ship's sonar systems, from repairing and calibrating fathometers to submarine detection. It was cool.

One of the trouble-shooting protocols they taught was called, "Half-Splitting". When a system failed, cut it in half and determine if it worked up to that point. You keep repeating the process until you identify the intersection of failure. We can apply a similar technique to personality design assessment. I like to start by half-splitting the assertiveness continuum. Assertiveness is usually easy to see. It manifests itself in verbal and nonverbal behaviors like the pace of speech, attire and body language.

Body language is so important, look for clues as soon as possible. Sustaining a level of sensitivity to body language and nonverbal queues is essential. By the way, how are yours? Are you meeting confidence with confidence in your nonverbal approach? Are you toning it down when it's coming in too hot? Are you at pace with pace? Receiving excitement with excitement? In your own way! Don't sprain your sense of self trying to "fit in." It's about purposeful versatility. It's being a great interpersonal dancer that makes his or her partner look amazing. It's being a servant leader, taking the first step, extending grace and accommodating needs. It's meant to honor and edify others.

What I have observed (as indicated in the illustration), is a difference in operating frequencies on either side of the *Assertiveness Meridian*. As assertiveness decreases, frequency decreases. As assertiveness increases, frequency increases. The *Controller* and *Creator* operate at a higher frequency than the *Calculator* and *Connector*. The responsiveness of the *Controller* and *Creator* makes them each emotionally unique, but they share this higher operating frequency.

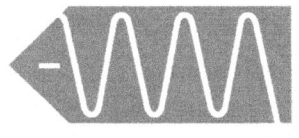
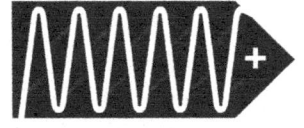

13a. Operating Frequency effects assertiveness

Conversely, the *Calculator* and *Connector* operate at a lower frequency. Their rate of speech is usually slower and more deliberate than the hyper *Creator* or the Tell mode *Controller*. The *Calculator* is methodical in their loyalty to the process and the need to think through decisions carefully, it's a slower decision process. Low frequency isn't bad! After all, "It's all about the bass." Yeah, the rhythm section, man! It's just the different designs operating at their own frequencies, with all of their organic strengths and weaknesses in play.

The Frequency model quickly gives us an idea what side of the meridian we are approaching. Try to visualize the delta between your design and theirs. What side of the meridian are you on? Do you need to increase your frequency a bit? Create a faster cycle? Or slow it down and let it breathe? This is *Taking It To The Bridge*! Making that first move to extend beyond your default approach and purposefully connect.

We will delve deeper into the subject of tools specific to each personality design as we proceed. For now, our objective is to quickly assess the personality design we are engaging. The next quick call is on responsiveness, or emotional regulation. This is making the call between Spock and Bones for you Star Trekkers out there (I know Roddenberry said Trekkies but...) Let's take our half-splitting approach to responsiveness.

In the regions North of the Responsiveness Parallel, the *Calculator* and *Controller* live in a world colored by their task or project-oriented design. They ask questions about, "What" and *When* as a priority, not, *Who*. That would be the role of people-centric, emotionally open responders. The *Connector* and *Creator*, despite their different frequencies, both agree—it starts and ends with *people*.

This early call on responsiveness is valuable. It will help us get into the exchange gracefully, building trust and creating comfort. Is small talk being encouraged by his or her open relaxed demeanor, or is it moving right to business after a cordial hello? In this perspective we are stepping toward emotional equalization. Not parity, just closing the gap.

EMOTIONAL RESPONSIVENESS

CONTROLLERS,
CALCULATORS
= LESS
EMOTIONAL

ASKS "WHAT"

**CREATORS,
CONNECTORS
= MORE
EMOTIONAL**

ASKS "WHO"

13b. What vs. Who

Use the half-splitting technique to quickly determine someone's personality design. Remember, it's situational and stress plays a role, so there may be contextual subtleties to consider. Draw from nonverbal cues, the pace and content of the conversation. High Frequency cadence and rich dialogue around who and how amazingly cool it was? *Creator.* Low frequency cadence and lots of questions about what and how? *Calculator.* We know where we are on the möbius, and now we know where *they* are. It's time to close the gap.

Applied Versatility

One small step for mankind, one interpersonal leap for mankind…or something like that. Regardless, Neil Armstrong was right, the first step is monumental. We need to be willing to take that first step if our goal is elevated interpersonal effectiveness. We need to take that first step, and the one after, and the one after that. It's on us, and do not expect reciprocal behavior! That's right, do not expect others to do the same just because you do it. Don't advertise the fact you are trying harder to meet others interpersonal needs and preferences. This is a personal journey and like parenting it often feels thankless, but like parenting it also creates abundance that is hard to express. The *Rock Your Gig* perspective is an elevated perspective. It challenges us to be self-aware while curating the health of our precious, personal ecosystem. It inspires us to shed illusions of the status quo, to be curious and take accountability. These are mature perspectives. It takes maturity, confidence and grace to step outside of your personal comfort zone. It takes grace to turn the other cheek when words become weapons.

Applied versatility is the willingness to take the first step, to extend an interpersonal bridge and walk toward the needs and preferences of *others first*.

Too heavy? Ok, it's like catching a raw egg, you need to match its trajectory and speed, and grasp it with a light touch. That's called, "success." Or, you can stand firm and end up with egg all over your face.

Navigating the Personality Design Möbius

The *Rock Your Gig* process always starts with self-assessment. It's the classic "check yourself before you wreck yourself." In that spirit, let's begin by identifying some of the tension points unique to each of the personality designs. If you don't know where you fall on the möbius at this point it's Ok. Objectively plotting your coordinates on the möbius can be a lot harder than we think. It's hard to imagine how disconnected we can be from how others see us. For now, adopt the design with which you feel the most connected.

Tension points are just those behavioral characteristics that sometimes challenge others. They can be mildly irritating or they may drive people to the brink of insanity! It's us, being us, our perfect design at work and play. We are focusing on these tension areas for the sake of self-awareness. We want a better picture of how others may see us. The *Rock Your Gig* philosophy is clear: You and your design are perfect. We are all exactly who we are in all our glory. Perfect in our imperfection.

My career as Fender's Chief Product Strategist can be traced by an unending stream of conversations and directives focused on how we could "fix" the iconic, legendary, Stratocaster® guitar. The very symbol of rock'n'roll. The instrument's design has its peculiarities, so on the surface, opportunities appear to abound. What people initiating these conversations didn't understand is it's everything that's *wrong* with the guitar that makes it so freaking right! And you my friend, are exactly the same. Don't ever think about changing who you are at your core, but seek versatility—the hallmark of the beautiful Stratocaster![26]

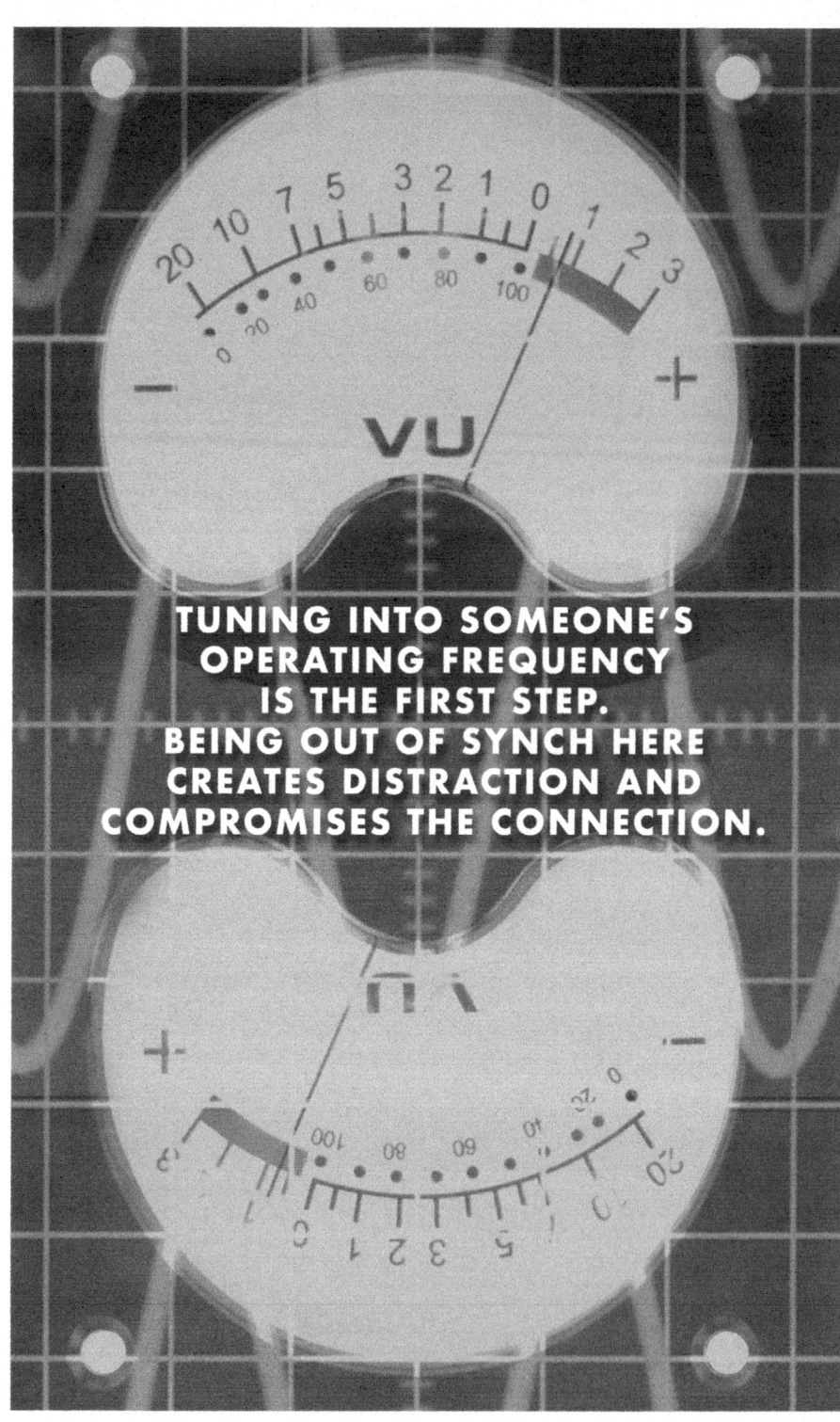

TUNING INTO SOMEONE'S OPERATING FREQUENCY IS THE FIRST STEP. BEING OUT OF SYNCH HERE CREATES DISTRACTION AND COMPROMISES THE CONNECTION.

CHAPTER 14

TENSION POINTS

CHAPTER 14.

TENSION POINTS

TENSION POINTS: THE CONTROLLER

Closed Body Language

Aggressive Pace and Posture

Poor Listener

Impatient

Unemotional = Uncaring

Oversimplification

It's a good thing your skin is so thick, you might mistakenly take this personally! These are all areas where the *Controller* should exercise awareness. The area that requires customization on your part is based on the design you are engaging. Disagreements between two *Controller* designs, for example, can be hard to resolve; each holding their ground because they, "Know what needs to be done."

The assertiveness of the *Controller* can dominate conversations and intimidate and stifle the *Connector* and *Calculator*. Slow down, open up, think about people a little and listen. Don't let your strengths get in your way and undermine your success! Focus and customize them to optimize interpersonal connectivity. Don't be so rigid, loosen your metaphoric tie, and if you actually wear a tie, yes—loosen it. Women, kick off your power heels and stay focused, just for a second. Productivity will barely be impacted by your lack of urgency. Just for a moment, for the sake of connection, lighten up.

ENGAGEMENT: THE CONTROLLER

• The Controller: Frequency

Tuning into someone's operating frequency is the first step. Being out of sync here creates distraction and compromises the connection. The *Controller* has a high operating frequency. The *Creator* will resonate with them easily, but the *Calculator* and the *Connector*, west of the Assertiveness Meridian, will need to increase their frequency to close the gap. This might include ramping-up the pace of your speech to accommodate. Get to the point as directly as possible, brevity rules the day.

• The Controller: Body Language

Controllers have a more reserved, laminated demeanor. Their posture may be assertive, leaning in on conversations, but they don't use emotional sign language and are distracted by it. *Creator*, put your hands in your pockets. *Calculator* and *Connector*, you may need to tighten it up a bit. The *Controller* can perceive others as loose and undisciplined. Be ready for a firm handshake and look them in the eyes.

• The Controller: Getting in the Moment—Gracefully

Be appreciative of the *Controller's* time. Don't start with small talk. Remember to keep your conversation focused on "what" and "when." Clearly state the reason for the meeting and the anticipated outcome. Short and sweet. If you have documents, offer them with a brief description of purpose. Don't float, be focused with the *Controller*, right from the outset.

• The Controller: Having the Moment—Effectively

The *Controller* operates from a base of "I know." They want to make a conclusion, to define a point of view. They need information to do that, but they are not usually interested in the fine detail. *Calculator*, you need a killer executive summary approach with the *Controller*. It doesn't matter if it's your boss or your son, the *Controller* design wants the essence not the ingredients. Present options to the *Controller* and let them decide.

Stay out of emotional dialogue with the *Controller*, it's way outside of their comfort zone. Don't ask them how something made them feel; stick to *what, when* and the *result*. The *Controller* is like that George Thorogood song, *"When I Drink Alone, I Prefer to Be By Mysef"*[27] Give them the tools and resources they need to work independently.

Pay attention, take notes, be deliberate and respectful of their time. The *Controller* likes to punch holes in new ideas. They are pressure testing them. This can put off and turn off the *Calculator* and *Connector*, don't let that pressure testing do that to you! Stay in there, sword fight for a bit. Let the *Contoller* get to, "I know."

Parents, your *Controller* child is cut from the same personality design cloth. Just because they are young doesn't change things a whole lot. Actually, their behavioral characteristics are unfiltered and pure.

• The Controller: Closing the Moment—With Clarity

Your goals with the *Controller* are *alignment* and *credibility*. You want to be precise but it's the forest, not the trees. Review succinctly from your notes, it shows respect and focus. Be observant, there are opportunities in the last phase for commonality. This can be a key to unlocking credibility with the *Controller*. End your conversation as purposefully as it began.

As a general rule, keep your sensitivities up when you're engaged with any of the 4Cs. The mistake I frequently observe is best described as a, "lack of instinct." We can come into interpersonal exchanges with a script and expectations that don't always pan out. Applied versatility requires the awareness to make a course change when it's needed.

The *Controller* doesn't offer a lot of emotional cues, you have to pay attention and look for signs. Former Fender CEO Bill Schultz was a *Controller* design. He would take his arms off the table, and lean back in his chair, looking up at the ceiling. I knew I had very little time to get to the point and wrap it up.

In business situations, you may need to prepare a succinct review. Apply the same logic—short and to the point. Don't put the *Controller* on whimsical e-mail threads, take them off. I used to twitch when I opened an email that said, "Thanks." You don't have to thank me, it's like that Mitch Hedberg[28] monologue, *"I'll give you the money, you give me the donut, end of transaction."* For the *Controller*, time is a precious commodity.

TENSION POINTS: THE CREATOR

Unorganized

Unfocused

Emotional Landslide

Missing Details

Self-Promoting

Impulsive

Creator, you too can dominate the conversation with your assertive, emotive manner. The *Calculator* and *Controller* can get frustrated by your lack of focus and attention to detail. "Squirrel!" The emotionally charged energy that inspires can be too much at times and lack appropriateness. You love the spotlight. Yes, you do. Give the microphone back. You love the spotlight and forget to share it with others. The people that did the work. You want to be recognized as an inspirational, unique leader and can appear to be running for office, selling yourself. "

I call it out, because it's me. I can speak with authority because today I am more aware of my *Creator / Controller* design and its strengths and weaknesses. If you are a *Creator*, you may need to slow down and turn down, get up to speed on the details, make room for others to speak, don't let your passion get the best of you. Focus on the task and drop the mic!

ENGAGEMENT: THE CREATOR

• The Creator: Frequency

The *Creator* like the *Controller* is on the high frequency side of the möbius. The *Connector* and *Calculator* will need to adapt to their fast pace. The *Creator* moves fast, thinks fast, talks fast and loses focus just as fast. You don't need to match their frequency, just be ready for it and embrace it. The *Creator* will naturally want to pull you up to their enthusiasm level. Let them. They are trying to inspire, show them it's working.

• The Creator: Body Language

The *Creator* is passionate and emotional, not the natural fit for the *Calculator* and *Controller*. They are very people-sensitive and "feel" their way through life. If you're in the North regions of *Calculator* and *Controller* responsiveness, you will need to open your body language a bit, there could be a hug in your future (not saying in won't be awkward, but don't be put off). The *Creator* will read you, be prepared. Be happy to see them, it makes them feel good.

• The Creator: Getting in the Moment—Gracefully

Don't be mad if they are late. Take your time, there is room for small talk focused on "Who" and feelings. Unlike the *Calculator* and *Controller,* look for commonality on the front side, during this more improvised segment, versus at the conclusion of the engagement. Greet the *Creator* like the inspiring, unique individuals they are. The *Creator* is a celebrity, so give them an emotional round of applause when you see them.

• The Creator: Having the Moment—Effectively

The *Creator* doesn't manage the details well. This is something you can bring to the relationship. They appreciate the collaboration and see it as supporting their cause. The *Creator* feeds off the creative exchange, so don't bring fully baked ideas, bring concepts and leverage their creativity.

The *Creator* often flies by the seat of their pants, or perhaps the seat of their active-wear. They won't reject your organizational support.

The *Creator* needs to bring people into the conversation. The Creator wants to talk "Who", they want to know the people involved. The teachers, the other students, the design team, the attorneys, whoever participated.

To the *Creator*, all the world's a stage, so bring the band down behind them and let them shine. Use acknowledging gestures to show support as they share. Keep your body language energized and engaged.

Be ready for an emotional response to bad news. Personal attacks are not out of the question. You have to make room for excess emotional energy with the *Creator*.

Share, dream and collaborate with the *Creator*. That's what they will remember, you and the richness of your ideas and passion for them. Less emotive personality designs need to find safe, comfortable ways to open up and take a brainstorm approach with the *Creator*.

• The Creator: Closing the Moment—With Clarity

The *Creator* is assertive so give them options when decisions are required. Restate the highlights of your conversation and seek acknowledgment and alignment. Take notes when in business environments with the *Creator*, things can change in their minds and they may even need to be reminded what the plan was in the first place.

Leave any materials you compiled on their behalf, thank them for sharing the vision. Conversations with the *Creator* can get loose and lose focus. Acknowledge the full range of the conversation, not just the points that mattered to you. Respect their creative view.

There are more opportunities for commonality as conversations end with the *Creator*. They like to talk about themselves, what they are up to, who they are hanging out with. The *Calculator* and *Controller* will need to slow down and let the transition happen organically, it can be a long and opportunistic goodbye.

Keep good notes and follow up with a fully landscaped summary. The *Creator* sees this as positive support of their mission. They want to share your testimony—If it's good.

The young *Creator* is forming their sense of self and needs positive acknowledgment from adults when they color outside the lines. *Calculator* and *Controller,* don't be critical; conclude every creative showcase with support and enthusiasm. Feed their special gift.

TENSION POINTS: THE CONNECTOR

Unmotivated

Slow

Passive / Aggressive

Conflict Averse

Indecisive

Lack Focus

Oh man, I feel bad even delivering the news. Yes, even the nicest people on earth are complicated. Your lower operating frequency makes you look like you're moving in slow motion to the *Controller* and *Creator.*

"If you choose not to decide, you still have made a choice."

This is an appropriate contextual lyric by the band, *Rush* and lyricist / drummer, the late great Neil Peart[29]. The *Connector's* lack of decisiveness can be seen as wishy-washy and non-committal to others. There is always a little tension created by this aspect of the *Connector's* Personality Design. *Connectors* are advised to embrace their design, but not turn away from opportunities to participate in decision making. Your kind, caring approach can be non-forthcoming if you think someone will be affected by your transparency.

The *Connector* needs to amp-up their frequency when dealing with *Controllers* and *Creators.* Sit-up and lean-in. Focusing on what, how and when. Make a recommendation! What, am I insane? Yes, think of it as a friendly assertion that could easily become a decision. Don't change, please don't change, we love you just the way you are, just pick up the pace a bit.

ENGAGEMENT: THE CONNECTOR

• The Connector: Frequency

Connectors, like fellow *Calculators* operate in the lower frequency zone to the West of the Assertiveness meridian. If you're from the other side of the tracks, you will need to slow down to match their pace. It isn't a question of good or bad, it's simply *high* or *low*. If you are spinning like a drone, *Connectors* will be intimidated. Match their steady, calm cadence and create a safe environment.

• The Connector: Body Language

Connectors are reserved but open in their demeanor. They don't use the overt emotional expressions that Creators do, but they feel as deeply. Nonverbal cues are key, Assertive Designs can easily intimidate them unknowingly. Eye contact is good, but occasionally look away. Stay open, match their relaxed posture. Look for their hands to indicate comfort. Fidgeting with hair, mouth and ears can be subtle signs to turn it down a bit. Or it could be allergies. Geeez, lighten up.

• The Connector: Getting in the Moment—Gracefully

Connectors are easy to talk to. They find *Controllers* to be intimidating, they want to trust *Creators* with their feelings, but they know that can backfire. Warmth and sincerity are the best policy with *Connectors*. Start easy if you're Assertive, think *Who* not *What*. Ease into the conversation with a few pleasantries. Be interested, not Interesting.

• The Connector: Having the Moment—Effectively

The challenge with the *Connector* is creating urgency without causing them to fold up shop. They don't like pressure so soften your approach. You want to know where they are with the project, but you need to start with how they are *feeling* about it.

Ask for their opinion, they will be honored. Share and solicit ideas from them, don't judge the validity, just listen. Find out what they "like" about the project, talk team. Do they have any concerns or doubts? You want to mine their feelings and people-centric sensitivity. They know a lot about the "health of the patient."

Look to create mutual agreement. Don't dictate, don't push, keep it light but try to keep it focused and on track. Let it meander a bit. If you are a *Controller* or *Calculator*, make room for feelings, people and team. Match your frequency, turn down a bit, slow down and smell the roses.

The *Connector* leads with their heart, your engagement needs to sustain an element of safety, comfort and trust. Credibility comes when they see your aim is true. The *Connector* is concerned about the feelings and opinions of others. They need to know you are happy, he's happy, she's happy, everyone is happy, and everything is awesome, when you're part of the team!

• The Connector: Closing the Moment—With Clarity

Closing an engagement with the *Connector* needs to be seamless; let the transition be as organic as possible. Don't send the *Connector* out for a spacewalk; keep them tethered to others in collaboration. A great way to create positive connectivity when exiting an engagement is to bring others in as a next step or roll up your sleeves and collaborate with them. The *Connector* wants to—you guessed it, *connect* with you.

When restating the meeting's outcomes, use team speak—"We like option A, right?" Help them decide through partnership. If you don't purposefully close the conversation with the *Connector* things can drift. "Should I reach out to Elizabeth, or do you want to?" Help them get organized.

Look for commonality with the *Connector* through people talk. Mutual friendships, shared interest in sports teams, celebrities and people in the news. These can be relevant starters for your next conversation. Be interested, listen and learn a little more every time.

Thank the *Connector* for their time, their ideas, their partnership and for sharing their feeling about the issues. Verbalize your appreciation, thank them for their support. Thank them again when you send a note highlighting the decisions you arrived at together.

TENSION POINTS: THE CALCULATOR

Indecisive

Critical

Unemotional = Uncaring

Avoid Conflict

Detached

Unenthused

Calculator, your methodic approach and the need to be correct can keep you from pulling the trigger. The *Controller* and *Creator* will say you have "analysis paralysis." Your tendency to reschedule conflict (seemingly forever), erodes trust and diminishes credibility. Your demeanor is relaxed and confident, but combined with your less responsive emotional profile, you can appear unenthused, detached and distant. Your resistance to mid-flight changes can be seen as rigid and unsupportive.

Come out and talk, the questions can wait. Realize perfection can be the enemy of progress. Everything isn't logical. There is no logical reason why my wife married me, but thank heaven she did. Show interest in the performance not just the process. Sometimes history tells us nothing about the present. Look up, lighten up, speed up, speak up and smile.

ENGAGEMENT: THE CALCULATOR

- **The Calculator: Frequency**

The *Calculator* operates in the low frequency zone. They are measured and somewhat linear in their approach. They blend well with the *Connector* in their natural cadence, but struggle matching the high frequency approach of the *Controller* and *Creator*. Their operating frequency is closely tied to the underlying process. *Controller* and *Connector*, adjust your frequency down a notch.

• The Calculator: Body Language

Reserved. Tune in to their introspective style. Slow your speech down, lower the volume a bit and most importantly leave open space for them to think before they respond. If you rush this process they will close down. The *Calculator* is measured and organized, and this is reflected in their demeanor. *Creator,* put your hands in your pockets and give them personal space.

• The Calculator: Getting in the Moment—Gracefully

Don't make small talk unless it's invited. Be appreciative of their time and expertise. The *Calculator* is always untying knots, there is always something challenging being tackled. Show interest, ask questions that set a tone of respect for their expertise. Focus your off-task conversations on *What* versus *Who*. Be interested in what they are working on. Look for commonality in technology and the sciences.

• The Calculator: Having the Moment—Effectively

The *Calculator* is organized and prepared and you will get off to a bad start if you're not. They typically have a serious and purposeful demeanor you will need to match to be taken seriously. Earning credibility with the *Calculator* will come not by what you know, but by acknowledging what you don't know. You'll engage the *Calculator* with curiosity and interest in their field of expertise.

Focus your energy on understanding the process of the *Calculator*. They will tell you exactly where you currently are, and the challenges and caution required to complete the mission with precision and the desired outcome. Understand that their deadlines are like budgets; they are a goal, but they can be fluid. Maxims like, "The process will tell us when we are done" may emerge from the mouth of the *Calculator*. They can frustrate the heck out of the other personality designs, but to them, anything that subverts the process is jeopardizing the mission, Dave!

Take notes, listen carefully and let the conversation breathe.

A lot happens in the open spaces with the Calculator, they are formulating a point of view; if you press past it before they get done, they stop and hit reset. You will never get anywhere, and they become frustrated and reschedule you in their priorities. Ask questions and wait (sometimes in awkward silence), for what feels like way too long. That's when you know you're doing it right with the *Calculator*.

Controller, try not to come across as too decisive, you may not have all the details they do. You will end up back peddling. Come to them seeking answers, not delivering them. Revere their capacity for precision and excellence, revere the process.

• The Calculator: Closing the Moment—With Clarity

Organization rules the day so don't over-simplify in your efforts to synthesize the outcome. If you are both *Calculators*, take the time to fill in the details, you'll both feel better. All other designs, I would encourage you to solicit the review from them or send a draft for them to edit. You will miss things that are important to them in the details, so defer to their expertise organizing and systematically executing the details.

When things are off track don't press for a new deadline at the meeting's conclusion. They can't respond until the process reveals the answer to them. They aren't going to guess. It's like asking the copier tech when they think they will be done; "You'll know when I'm done because I won't be here."

Honor and edify everyone when you have shared time with them. The *Calculator* wants to be appreciated for their expertise and commitment to getting the job done right. Honor them for their unique abilities. This is equally true with a young *Calculator*. Feed their passion for doing things right; play chess with them, give them responsibilities that reflect your confidence in their skills and help them use logic and process to make decisions. Leave space for them to think. End on a positive note of confidence in their capabilities and support for the process.

You made it, congratulations! Let's take a minute to regroup and get ready to Rock.

CHAPTER 15

GO FORTH AND ROCK

CHAPTER 15.

GO FORTH AND ROCK

Rehearsals are over and tomorrow is the big show. It's time to put it all together and Rock Your Gig. The first thing we need to do in preparation, is formalize the run-of-show and write a killer set list that leaves the audience wanting more. We have a bunch of cool new riffs to showcase, and a better appreciation for the other players in the band. All good stuff.

To insure we don't miss an opportunity to rock, let's sketch out the day like a Stage Manager or Operations VP might. Trust me, they may sound like completely different roles, but they are absolutely the same guy, just one has longer hair, gaffers tape, and a chatty walkie-talkie. The point is, they both care a lot about the details, and so should you. If it isn't formalized, written down as an intentional plan, it isn't real. It doesn't matter if it's a stage plot or your career vision. You have to bring it to life. Let me present a little more form and dimension to the process.

Our goal is to intentionally leverage all five elements of the *Rock Your Gig* philosophy, as often as possible.

To review:

> **1. The Spirit of Reinvention**
>
> **2. The Ecosystem of You**
>
> **3. Objective Self-Assessment**
>
> **4. Understanding Others**
>
> **5. Effective Communication**

We have been on a diverse and thought-provoking journey. Our tendency is to remember the early chapters and the book's ending, and drop the pieces in the middle. We don't want to lose the forest for the proverbial trees. If we put purposeful energy into these five principals, we will elevate our individual performance. When we elevate, we become more visible. We generate more energy which translates as positive differentiation.

Our personal brand becomes more clearly defined and increases in value. As time progresses, our cache of positive connections with others fills. Our coworkers appreciate how we relate to them, and they want to see us win. The crowd goes wild, chants for an encore fill the stadium, and you my friend, get promoted.

I know this approach works because I did it this way. I was promoted ten times in twenty-five years. I started in an entry level position at thirty-five years old, with only a high school diploma and made it to the C-Suite in ten years. So, I absolutely believe you can energize your career progression if you make a conscious effort to apply these five principals. Let's look at each in practical application. It is important to remember, each of these five elements are independent *and* interconnected forces. As you invest in one area, there is a positive-compounding effect across the whole of your personal ecosystem.

1. THE SPIRIT of REINVENTION—ON STAGE

Tomorrow is a new day. What needs to be different? How bold is your vision? What areas of your life do you want to focus on? Unless you have been knocked to the ground by the need to evolve, subtle opportunities to leverage reinvention can be hard to see. Pull out your self-assessment survey from Chapter 3; are there any areas that look opportunistic? Here are some ideas to help you visualize what Reinvention might look like tomorrow. Strap in!

• Wakeup Call

- What time are you getting up tomorrow? Do you want to start a new habit and add a couple hours to your day? If you did, get up a little earlier, how could you invest that time? It seems ridiculous, I know, but this simple change can fuel unbelievable growth. You may need to go to bed a little earlier. If you are just spending quality time with your couch in the evening, go to bed so you can add a few productive hours to your morning. Adding just two hours a day creates over seven hundred hours of bonus time to your year. If you have a five year plan you can invest the equivalent of ninety-one, forty-hour work weeks into your endeavor.

- **Make Your Bed**

If you want to set a positive, productive tone to your day, right out of the gate, make your bed. It's a simple mechanic, but it represents a level of personal discipline and productivity. It's a result, it's picking up after yourself. If this is an opportunity for you, then set a goal to make your bed every day for a month. You might think I am nuts at this point, but I am absolutely serious.

The power of reinvention is its ability to knock us out of the swirling orbit of the status quo. It's not *the man* keeping us down, it is *us* keeping us down! When we put a new productive practice like this in place, even a simple one like making our bed, it starts a cascading chain reaction, like dominoes falling. It's a micro-tipping point that you initiate.

- **Look in the Mirror**

What do you see? Are you ready for a new look? Are you ready to see something fresh in your reflection? What does your personal brand look like today? What do you want it to look like tomorrow? Our personal demeanor and attire starts broadcasting what we are about before we ever say a word. Is it time to change the message you are sending? If you were to elevate your demeanor, what updates would you make? Today's the day, do it, make the change.

- **Meditation**

Add a fifteen-minute meditation to your morning routine. This is your opportunity to script your day. Cleanse your mental pallet, shut down your left brain for a minute, and get into the moment. Our sub-conscience mind is often littered with junk mail, negativity, and cognitive distortions. Meditation puts us back in control of our emotional state. It allows us to regulate and reprogram our thoughts which, in turn, colors our mood, behavior and attitude. We don't wake up in a bad mood, our thoughts *put us there*. So, take control of your thoughts and meditate. Affirm your reinvention. Affirm your success and visualize your promotion. Meditation may also reveal other opportunities for reinvention, growth, and fulfillment.

• Nutritional Kick-Start

What are you having for breakfast? Is it an opportunity to bring some balance to the ecosystem? Try this tomorrow; drink a big glass of water when you wake up. Just water. I am blown away at how many people I know that don't drink water, let alone start their day by refueling with the essence of life. You are made of water, don't make your internal organs work overtime to scrub and filter everything you swallow. Have your coffee later.

After your meditation, sit down and eat a piece of fruit. If you have to run, grab it to go. Fruit comes in a convenient package; easy and healthy. Avoid eating fruit after other solid foods. It ferments in your gut while it waits for slower digesting foods to break down. Then eat a sensible lunch at your regular time.

Water—Meditation—Fruit—Refuel. It's ok to get a little hungry before you eat. As a matter of fact, it's better if you do, just don't overeat when you eventually sit down, as a result. This cadence will create a 14 to 18-hour gap between your big meals. Your engine will run smoother, you will enhance the balance of your ecosystem, and produce more positive energy.

• Attire

What are you wearing today, and do you want to make any changes? Our individuality is so important to us. Sometimes, however, it can get in our way. My career advice is to dress like the individuals that have the roles you want. It's about fit, it's tribal, you're in a band—is it *Nirvana* or the *Boston Philharmonic*?

• Promptness

Get to work *on time*. Get there before your supervisor. If you are perpetually late, then engineer yourself out of this bad habit. At some point you have decided that it's ok to be late. Either because you are a disorganized victim, or you believe what you are doing is more important than where you are supposed to be. This is an opportunity to neutralize a negative differentiator.

• Exercise

Add an exercise ritual to your day. The investment in your physical health will bring energy to interpersonal exchanges. Take a walk in the morning, take a walk at lunch, buy some hand weights. Don't let gym memberships, time or money be an excuse. Just start as small as you have to, but do start.

Here is a page out of my own history for your consideration. During the course of my cancer treatments, I was constantly getting IVs set and blood drawn. They would have to stick me multiple times, in multiple places, then call in a phlebotomy ninja to get it done. I filed it under "things that suck." I was telling my oncologist that I was absolutely fatigued by the process and he made a suggestion. He said, "Why don't you buy one of those spring resistance hand grips and pump up your veins before your tests." I was desperate and it made sense, so I did.

I started doing it before my test, then I started doing it in the back of the Uber on the way to work, then I started doing it more, and more, and more. Two years later, I was lifting weights at home before work three days a week. I lost a hundred pounds, reduced my pain levels and got stronger. A six-dollar set of hand grips triggered life enhancing reinvention. Just start, do it *today*.

• Positivity

Design a more positive persona. I did something years ago that to this day remains a defining element of my personal brand. I set a personal goal to issue an over the top, positive response anytime someone asked me, "How's it going?" My favorite response is an energetic, "Awesome." said with conviction and a smile. People are genuinely impacted by this simple choice. Yes choice. It's easy for me to say, "I am awesome, how are you?", because I choose awesomeness, purposefully. It's authentic. The other thing that it does is short circuit negative exchanges before they start. Don't fall into the, "I had a shitty weekend." conversations. This is not a winning attitude and will bring you down. Your goal is to elevate above the crowd and be recognized by your excellence.

- **Make an Agreement With Yourself**

Define and formalize your intentions to reinvent. Create succinct verbal statements you can say as one of your affirmations. Create a physical Vision Board of images depicting your new reality, success, and happiness. Make it up and make it happen.

These are just a few ideas for you to consider. The variables and individual opportunities are boundless. My goal is to stimulate your passion to seek change that elevates your life and your professional profile. Give yourself permission to redesign your look, your attitude, your environment, your influences, and your life.

Reinvention is the catalyst of growth. I began simply playing an instrument. My passion for it led me to a career designing and marketing instruments. The final stage of my reinvention occurred when I became an instrument. An instrument of honor and grace, an instrument of inspiration, creativity, and excellence. This was core to my overall success, fulfillment and happiness and will serve you as well.

Close your eyes and imagine your new reality—see it clearly, know it's possible, bring it to life by taking the first step *today*.

2. THE ECOSYSTEM OF YOU—ON STAGE

As you know, I use this as a metaphor to describe the system and interdependent functionality of our lives. Our physical, emotional, and spiritual selves, and the external world around us. A balanced, healthy personal ecosystem brings energy, clarity and focus to our interpersonal encounters. You have to be ready to rock when you hit the stage, or the conference room.

- **Take the Life Balance Assessment** (page 58)
This will help you identify target opportunities and prioritize

them. Be honest with yourself and consider asking your partner or a trusted friend for their opinions. Examine what areas could use focus, and don't entertain any limiting excuses. Recall our conversation on *Situational Analysis* in Chapter 2 and look for ways to merge activities.

This holistic perspective recognizes the impact of our physical, emotional, and spiritual balance. If you don't believe that these elements have any influence on your career advancement, you are mistaken. Let's take an extreme example to make a point. You and your friends enjoy an epic evening of libations. You get home pretty late and when the alarm goes off—oh man, you realize you feel like a dive bar dumpster. You get up, get dressed and head to work. Maybe a burrito on the way to help sop up the toxins. What you are bringing through the door is *not* going to impress anyone! This is an extreme example but makes the point.

Creating a healthy, balanced personal ecosystem is critical to sustaining long term success. We have to be healthy, emotionally balanced and inspired to compete and win. If we walk around under a dark cloud due to an emotional or spiritual imbalance, people will not be attracted to us. Well, that isn't completely true. Other people under their own dark clouds will be enthused to mope and complain alongside us.

The goal is to create greater balance in our personal ecosystem. This will increase the quality of *all* our encounters. The challenge is finding the courage and motivation to question the status quo and break out with a new perspective; whether that is defined by society's expectations and norms, or our own limiting perspectives. Let's explore ideas to help us get in-touch and in-tune with our personal ecosystem.

• Physical Health creates positive energy

This is transmitted to others via our nonverbal gestures, posture, demeanor, personal appearance, smile, tension behaviors and attitudes. The laws of attraction apply. When you are vibrating at an elevated frequency, others operating at that frequency will be attracted to you. This leads to opportunities for collaboration with like-minded, energized people. If you are not doing it already, start making small investments in your physical health.

PHYSICAL HEALTH BOOST

• Take a Walk

I can't think of a better way to start the cycle of renewal. It's low impact, whole body and offers some elevated cardiovascular activity; blood and oxygenated muscles detoxifying your body and your mind. If you had a car and you parked it in your driveway for years, and you never took it for a spin, or even started it, can you imagine what a sad state it would be in? Guess what, your body is no different. Use it, or lose it, as the expression goes. The good news is our bodies have incredible regenerative powers. Start walking with dedication, it's a poetic way to start your journey to elevated physical health.

• Food

Nutritional awareness is another great topic to focus on. You owe it to yourself and your family to be informed. Snap out of the matrix and take a stand. I have already shared my perspectives on the importance of understanding what you are eating and where it came from. Is it science, or is it real food? You don't need a panel of doctors to confirm what too much sugar does to our kids—the manic, whacked-out and fatiguing behavior that is abruptly followed by a thirty-thousand foot drop. You know there are lunches that will put you just short of a coma. Food matters.

Set specific goals to learn more about nutrition. Watch a *Netflix* documentary on food with your partner. Form a point of view, don't just eat stuff because it's what you always eat. Stop and think about it. If you fuel your personal ecosystem with high quality nutrients it will respond with abundance. Increased energy, responsiveness and clarity can all be attained!

• Take Up A Sport

Sometimes the issue is finding an activity we can get excited about, something we enjoy. I am a tennis hound. I love tennis. My passion for tennis and my desire to get better inspired my health objectives. I didn't party or eat poorly on Friday night because I knew I was going to be playing Saturday morning.

Committing to a community program or hiring a trainer will help keep you honest and on track. It won't take long, typically about three weeks, and you will feel cheated when you don't get your activity time. Yoga, Pilates, repelling, hiking, martial arts, weight lifting, swimming, bike rides, frisbee golf; anything that makes your heart beat a little harder, and gets you off the couch.

• High Quality Rest

If you find it difficult to get quality rest, it may be a sign of something more serious. If you believe this is the case, seek professional assistance. If you are just burning the candle at both ends, stop. I used to stay up late every night, watching TV or on the web, because "I couldn't get to sleep", or so I told myself—and my wife. If you are trading screen time for rest, you are shortchanging your ecosystem in a big way. You have to work at it! Try going to bed a little earlier for a week or two, eventually you will change the pattern. You have to turn off the screens, the stimuli command your restlessness. You will have more energy, grace and versatility if you get quality rest.

• Meditation

Consider a second fifteen-minute meditation midday. Even a clumsy fifteen-minute session can be incredibly invigorating. Some days it honestly feels like a two hour nap. Try it for thirty days. You will never stop.

Let's not lose our way, the mission is—*Get Promoted*. Your brand can't illuminate and inspire confidence if it's weak and diffused. This is not about physical appearance! This is not about how much you weigh, how old you are, or what size shoe you wear. This is about your life energy and how people perceive it; how you shine and the clarity in your eyes, the bearing of your demeanor and the confidence you inspire.

• Emotional Health Fosters Positive Connectivity

The goal is elevated self-awareness and learning to regulate our emotional tides. The breadth and depth of emotional energy is staggering to consider. The highs can be stratospheric and the lows, soul crushing.

A word of encouragement if you are really struggling here and running out of ideas—please seek the aid of a professional counselor. Emotional health, self-esteem and a positive outlook are the super fuel of fulfillment, success, and happiness.

We can absolutely influence our emotional state. If you recall, it is our thoughts that color our emotions, or mood. Not the other way around. There are also bio-chemical triggers we can pull as well.

EMOTIONAL ENERGY BOOST

Let's explore opportunities to achieve a greater level of positive emotional energy, capacity, and balance within our personal ecosystem.

• Chemical Warfare

Endorphins are the body's natural Ecstasy. They activate the brain's opioid receptors to reduce pain levels, and create a feeling of euphoria. This wonder drug wasn't concocted by big pharma, it comes as standard equipment in your magnificent design. It was included free with your hypothalamus package. So, what's my point? *Get high before the gig—the natural way!* Set your endorphins loose!

• Exercise

Is a great way to fire up your endorphins. Once again, we see the interconnectivity within the ecosystem. In this case our physical investment is going to have positive influence on our emotional health. So, take a walk, work out, swim—get high.

• Acupuncture

Acupuncture and massage are both known to stimulate the production of endorphins.

• Chocolate

Or a glass of wine might do the trick. In moderation, and not before work or sleep!

- **Meditation**

Can be an effective source of positive emotional energy. The act of mindfulness, getting into the absolute moment can help relieve emotional stress.

- **Laugh and Smile**

Find a reason to laugh, hang around someone funny, listen to a comedy routine during your commute.

- **Cognitive Awareness**

Is the first step in learning to regulate our emotional responsiveness more effectively. These internal conversations color our stage-presence; they influence what the audience sees. I want to suggest an exercise to help get you moving in this direction tomorrow. The first step is to identify these dissonant notes in our conversations with others. To review: *All or Nothing Thinking, Over Generalization, Jumping to Conclusions, Emotional Reasoning* and *Magnification*. There are many other categories but for now let's focus our attention on these five.

You will be amazed at how many of these you collect in a day. It is easy to tell ourselves that this is just the way people talk—no, it's the way people THINK! It is likely the way you think from time to time as well. These little, seemingly harmless expressions create huge belief systems. They must be neutralized early. Ask yourself or your peer, "Is that really true? Does this actually 'always happen' or does it just feel that way?" Do not do this in an accusatory tone, even when you are talking to yourself!

It takes a road-case full of self-awareness to catch yourself falling into these cognitive webs. It may be easier to observe this behavior in others first, then reflect it on to yourself. I started by looking for just one that I felt was an opportunity for me, and easy to identify—*All or Nothing Thinking*. Keep your sensitivity on high for the words *never* and *always* when your peers or loved ones are accentuating their frustrations and challenges. Add another as time progresses, eventually you will become much more aware of these dangerous thoughts that distort and color your view of life and limit your true potential.

• The Morning Affirmation

Our thoughts need to be curated every day! They get twisted, jumbled and out of sync. While we sleep our subconscious mind has a house party, and we need to clean up the mess the morning after. Some days are more challenging than others. The longer we go without cleaning our inbox, the more diluted our focus becomes. These illusions can be weighty, and as time rolls on, they become a burden to carry and our progress halts.

Affirmations are incredibly effective at reprogramming our thoughts with positive empowering truths. Early on, I personally put up a ton of resistance to this practice, it just didn't feel... cool. Eventually I saw what it was doing in Lisa's life and I begrudgingly, and without expectations, gave it a try. Whoops! Boy, did I waste a lot of time. I wish I had started this years ago. It's common knowledge that the most successful athletes in the world visualize and affirm. Most of these incredible individuals cite their emotional preparation as much as their physical readiness for their success. We know this, but we struggle to understand how it might help us everyday folks.

You wouldn't just roll out of bed and jump on stage to perform, would you? Why should your job be any different? I am here to tell you Billy Shakespeare was right, the world is a stage, and you need to be in-tune, know your parts and looking good when the lights come up. Affirmations are your backstage ritual. Learn more about it, be a student. It's the perfect Life Hack to roll into your meditation practice. Create a positive, energized you that is ready to seize the next opportunity that presents itself.

• Spiritual Health

Seek an idea that humbles you. Something to honor beyond yourself. We are the only spiritual creatures on earth. It is an obvious gap in our being when it is unfulfilled. This is an essential element of achieving greater balance in your ecosystem. It pays quiet dividends over the long haul. It may give you a perspective that saves your life or repairs an important relationship. It's the invisible connective tissue between us all.

I saw a parallel in my business experience at Fender when

we moved to a more horizontal organization, or *Pods*. We abandoned the vertical alignment and organized into business units. Each group included *Category Merchants, Designers, Financial Analysts, Project Management* and related functions. The groups included a range of seniority from Coordinators to Vice Presidents, all sitting together in an open work area. Offices were turned into meeting spaces, and crumbled egos littered the floor.

What happened next changed the game forever. All these individuals lined up under the objective to serve it. It didn't matter what their rank was, they collaborated to ensure the success of the project. The project was King. The vision was bigger than any one individual's bias. Professionalism and respect were always part of the mix, but there was never a question about who we were serving. These teams went on to crush the competition. They became impenetrable, like a Roman legion marching in purposeful unison, hobnail boots pounding the marketplace with a relentless cadence. Our competitors could not match the focus, commitment, and organization we possessed as a team.

• Introspection
What ideals, values and beliefs guide your behaviors? Humans achieve greater balanced and are more in-tune with the universe when we represent and serve something bigger than ourselves. If you want to maximize your human potential, find greater measures of fulfillment, success, and happiness—fill the spiritual void, do it *now*.

3. OBJECTIVE SELF-ASSESSMENT—ON STAGE

Now let's see what leveraging your *Objective Self-Assessment* can look like in action. The four-part assessment offered in Chapter 3 will serve as the launch pad for this lifelong journey. The first two templates, *Getting Things Done* and *Strategic Energy*, are what I consider hard skills. These triggers are designed to reflect the traits needed to win at the *Business of Your Performance* in the areas of *Bridge Building* and *Influencing*

Others are soft skills required to win at the *Business of People!* You need both your head and your heart in the game if you want to *Rock Your Gig.*

Once you have completed the templates, identify one opportunity you would like to pursue within each of the four disciplines.

To illustrate, you may have identified *Collaboration* as an opportunity under the *Getting Things Done* field, and *Vision* as an opportunity in *Strategic Energy.* The process is then repeated in the soft skills arena as well. You may identify *Elevate Listening Skills* in the area of *Bridge Building* and become more consistent when attempting to influence others.

Don't pick easy things to work on, you may be sub-consciously avoiding the real issues that are holding you back. Don't make excuses that omit opportunities that seem out of reach.

- **Life Balance Assessment (revisited)**

Now take your formalized opportunity list and go back to your *Life Balance Assessment* template from Chapter 2. This is the compounding mechanic of the *RYG* philosophy. Let me walk you through one line of connectivity so that you can see the scope of intentional energy that can be applied to your objective.

We identified *Collaboration* as an opportunity for improvement in the area of *Getting Things Done.* As a leader I always had a place in my heart for people that got things done! Consistently and with a smile on their face. Put your completed *Life Balance Assessment* in front of you. Ask yourself this question, "What areas of focus would enhance my collaborative strengths?" If you scored low in the areas of *Friendships, Community* or *Serving* you may want to focus on those opportunities.

We must get to the root of what is keeping us tethered where we are. If you are not an assertive person and you find it difficult to initiate and invite collaboration, you may have the opportunity to develop those skills in a more indirect way. Planning a project with a friend or family member can bolster your appetite for partnership. Community service puts you right in the middle of collaborative scenarios. It will help you understand what it looks like, how to organize and rally support for your ideas, and work as a team.

The *RYG* philosophy believes the solutions to many of the challenges we face are within our reach. But there is no growth without resistance. We need to embrace our weaknesses and transform them into opportunities. In most cases, that simply means to stop ignoring them!

You know that being an energized, collaborative individual will increase your odds of career success. You know that your emotional, physical and spiritual energy can make it happen. Ask yourself, "How am I stacking the deck in my favor? How can I insure I am physically, emotionally and spiritually prepared for opportunities when they come my way?" Herein lies the magic —as soon as you begin preparing, elevating, and growing in earnest, positive things start happening. You don't have to stand on the curb waiting for opportunity; *opportunity starts looking for you!*

The investments you make in your physical, emotional and spiritual health will bring greater balance to your ecosystem. As the health and balance of your ecosystem increases, it's energy output increases—*and people notice!*

We are all connected by some unseen fabric. We sense other's energy, and they sense ours. But static energy becomes ambient noise to the community. It only responds to changes in the field of connectivity. When you invest, learn, and grow, your ecosystem creates a positive disruption. It's as if you had dropped a stone in a still pond; the rippling waves of energy expand indefinitely in every direction. These waves eventually connect with others in the grid that are operating at the same frequency. Things start to happen.

• Evaluate

All growth opportunities through the lens of your personal ecosystem first. In the poetic observations of blues legend, Willy Dixon— "If you want the fruit, you have to feed the roots." The roots of your success lie in a balanced and energized ecosystem.

• Peer Assessment

We discussed this in detail, but I want to come back and remind you to seek outside perspective. Copy the four *Applied Strengths* templates and ask a few carefully chosen people to share their perspectives. If you have a formal review process at your place of employment, all the better. Take their feedback and repeat the evaluation process through the ecosystem lens. Identify elements you believe will enhance your performance and capabilities and start investing. You have to start the cycle; you have to toss the stone. Hope is incredibly powerful, but it's a lousy career strategy.

4. UNDERSTANDING OTHERS—ON STAGE

• Know Your Audience

Up to this point we have been primarily focused on fine tuning our instrument and woodshedding new parts. Now it's time to jump on stage and jam with the band. We want to begin to apply our new understanding of Personality Designs as a way of increasing the effectiveness of our interpersonal encounters. Our goal is to understand and meet the unique needs and preferences of others—*first*. Here are a few ideas to kick-start the process.

• Build an Interpersonal CRM

High performing sales teams utilize a tool called a *CRM*, or *Customer Relationship Management* tool. It helps them to keep track of the unique needs and preferences of large numbers of customers. It's a way of building and sustaining intimacy, mining commonality and ultimately, building trust.

Savvy salespeople know that understanding the unique personality design of their potential customer could be the difference in closing a sale. They understand the weight and value of emotional intelligence. You can assume their superstar persona and approach your interpersonal encounters with the same intention. In this scenario you are the sales agent and the product you are selling is You!

The goal is to build a data base of the *Personality Designs* of your friends, family and peers. If the *CRM* analogy is a fit, and you interact with a large and diverse group of individuals then take that approach. If you are on a smaller team, or working in the home, you don't need to be as formal, but you need to make it real.

Start identifying the *Personality Designs* that offer the biggest challenges, and take a purposeful track toward improving those relationships. What is your plan to find commonality and what adjustments do you want to make to your approach, are good places to start.

• Plot Yourself In the Möbius

By now you should have a pretty good idea where you fall within the *Personality Designs* model. If you haven't done so, or you're still considering the details, you are likely a *Connector* or *Calculator*. Don't over think it! Focus on your assertiveness. As distorted as our self-reflection can be, most of us can place ourselves somewhere close to home. It's the situational variables that can throw us off track. Keep it loose for now. You will be taking the proactive posture and stepping out of your default zone to close the gap with others. If you don't know where you are starting from, that can be tough.

• Identify An Opportunity

What person or group in your ecosystem presents the biggest connectivity challenge/opportunity? Where are you struggling to connect? Is it the keyboard player? (I knew it!) What are some specific adjustments you might make to your approach? You have *Frequency, Responsiveness and Assertiveness* to consider. Search for commonality, contemplate your nonverbal messaging and theirs. Your goal is to formalize a new intentional approach.

This is a subtle, elevated, consistent approach to enhancing relationships. Be patient, look for meaningful opportunities to close the gap in authentic ways. Do not expect reciprocal behavior! Say it with me now, "Do not expect reciprocal behavior!" This is you holding yourself to a higher expectation. This is you building a bridge to close the gap—it's not a partnership. Don't be frustrated if you don't see a miracle overnight. Don't be disillusioned if you feel like it isn't working. Understand your energy is omnidirectional, you are dropping stones in the pond with every interaction. The energy is felt in the strange, hard to believe it's real, fabric that connects us all. Let me bring it down to earth for you. You can be building a bridge, placing the needs and preferences of another in front of your own, and failing miserably. Adjacent to your interaction are three people. These three people are moved and influenced by your approach. Do you see—you can't see! It takes faith. Stay on the high road, keep stepping out of your comfort zone when it's needed because it works in the big picture, where things happen.

• Be A Student

Interpersonal Effectiveness, Self-Assessment, Personality Designs, Emotional Intelligence, Cognitive Distortion, Meditation, Affirmation, The Laws of Attraction—all these tools, and many others are at your disposal. *RYG's* goal is to ignite your curiosity, inspire and empower you to seek higher ground. Be a student, your ecosystem thrives on this new energy. Expand the field of opportunity in your life, *Rock Your Gig* with knowledge.

5. EFFECTIVE COMMUNICATION—ON STAGE

• Communication Breakdown

This is where we bring all these elements into focus. None of this will matter until we are engaging others! How we communicate is the expression of the *RYG* philosophy. Everything we have discussed is about enhancing communication. Whether we are speaking to ourselves and the world through the *Spirit of Reinvention* or sitting down for a performance review, we are sending and receiving messages. As we have learned, we are even sending messages when we don't realize it.

Once again, I want to take you back to the topic of *Balance* in your personal ecosystem. This is the wellspring of energy behind your messaging. Are there any issues you see in your

Life Balance Assessment that might have material influence on the effectiveness of your communication? Is there anything surfacing in your *Applied Strengths Assessment* that stands out as an opportunity? Are your default behaviors aligned, in check and serving the need?

We want to follow the same line of thinking we used in the earlier *Collaboration* example. The goal is to identify contributing influences within our ecosystem that can help create an environment conducive for growth. It's always our first step. For example: If you see *Strategic Energy* as an opportunity, ask yourself what is supporting this goal in your *Life Balance Assessment* and what isn't. We know our physical health creates energy that will influence the strength and clarity of our messaging. We know our emotional wellbeing can be a factor. Do you have ideas, but lack the assertiveness to share them?

There has to be a clear line of sight, awareness and connectivity between your goals, your applied strengths and the contributing status of your ecosystem.

• Tune Your Body Language

Before you go onstage you need to make sure you are sending the right nonverbal message to the audience, so you warm-up in the green room and get ready to rock. Your gig is no different. Wake up tomorrow and check your nonverbal reflection. What is it telling the audience? Try doing this in your morning ritual and before any important meetings. What message do you want to send tomorrow when you walk through the door? Let the spirit of reinvention loose, elevate.

• Switching To Manual Mode

Put this to work for you immediately! There is no excuse to wait. It takes practice, so the sooner you begin the sooner you will Rock. To review—our default communication process is pretty simple and very automated. We are engaged in countless conversations across a variety of topics and mediums every day, from simple issues to complex matters of the heart. Most of these intersections are navigated on auto-comm. If you recall, our default automated system works something like this:

Witness: We take in stimuli and other's behaviors / messaging.

Conclude: Based on our experiences, *this* means *that*.

Reaction: *Fight* or *Flight* and everything in between.

Without overthinking this, on occasion we need to go manual, make a few quick assessments and customize our approach. Slow down and apply *Active Listening Skills*. Active listening is simply putting it all together. The words, the tone, the non-verbal expressions, environment, and the situational context.

• Mindfulness

Do not make any conclusions based on your emotional record keeping. Elevated communication requires *Mindfulness*. You need to be in the moment, engaged and seeking, to understand the needs and preferences of others—first. Our manual process looks something like this:

Witness: We take in stimuli and other's behaviors / messaging.

Assessment: Engage Active Listening.

Customize: Non-verbal gestures, tone and words.

Engage: Step outside default comfort zones / meet the need.

• Sustaining Communication Relevance

Our world continues to fragment. Unique problems require unique solutions. It's a customized, personalized, your-name-embroidered-here world. How we engage is not immune to evolution. How we communicate is often dictated by the technology we prefer to use. Some of us communicate across a variety of channels. The paradigm hasn't shifted, it's exploded into a fractal conversation.

The problem for many people is keeping up. Everyone has a different threshold for how many apps they want to absorb. Boomers, GenX and Millennial span the continuum of adoption. There are grandparents in future-shock and kids so technologically adept they appear bio-mechanical with their technological intimacy and fluidity.

The bottom line is this: We need to make an effort to keep up and ask for help if necessary. None of it is difficult, it's just new. We have to be comfortable communicating effectively across multiple channels today. We want to match the message to the medium to optimize understanding.

Set specific goals to get yourself over any technology barriers that are holding you back. You need to be able to leverage many mediums to connect in a relevant manner.

• Power Tools

Our primary focus has been on the soft skills that help us connect more effectively with the audience, our peers, friends and family. Now, let's examine a core business mechanic I have found to be underutilized by most young professionals that I coach. It's a simple and powerful differentiator that increases your visibility in a meaningful and professional way. It's hiding in plain sight, the tool is— *reporting*.

For some reason, reporting is easily overlooked as a method of enhancing communication, elevating your brand and creating positive, personal differentiation. We tend to have an attitude that says, "If someone wanted or needed a report, they would have asked me for it." This is one of those 1% moments; do you see it? This is why there is always room to move forward. If you want to *Rock Your Gig*, if you want to *Get Promoted* you can't think like the 99% club.

"Good afternoon Mr. Phelps, your mission, should you decide to accept it, is to identify an opportunity to organize, create and publish information related to your job via reporting." Actually, it's not *Mission Impossible*, it's really pretty simple. This advice is equally valid to new hires, young professionals or seasoned individuals—*anyone* that feels the need to break through and ignite career progression. Don't hesitate, this is something you can start today. Look for cross departmental collaboration opportunities as well.

- **Match the Message to the Medium, Situation and The Individual**

Consider creating a more formal communication strategy. When is an email the best solution, and when should you pick-up the phone and have a conversation? This becomes critical when you find yourself in damage control mode. We know our words are a small percentage of the effectiveness of our communication when it comes to sticky issues like beliefs and attitudes. If you are a *Connector* or *Calculator* design and less assertive by nature, you may want to avoid the conversation altogether. You need to know that about yourself and act accordingly. Be as thoughtful about what medium you choose as you are your words, your tone and demeanor.

EPILOG

The concept of communication is at the core of the *RYG* philosophy. It begins with an honest dialogue we have with ourselves, "What is working and what isn't?" We need to be able to communicate purposefully, clearly and consistently within ourselves to calibrate, align and dismantle subconscious illusions. When we allow negative self-talk into our ecosystem it weakens under the strain. If we can't articulate our beliefs, goals and strategies we cannot achieve them. When we don't express and reinforce our vision—it dissipates, and we surrender to defeat.

We communicate with every nuance of our being. Our posture, eyes, energy, attire, attentiveness, integrity, urgency, versatility, patience, passion, grace, and honor all speak on our behalf. It's important that we understand, refine and curate these indirect communications. It is the mass of these positive, aligned, consistent impulses, that increase the field of opportunity and ultimately creates a tipping point wherin good things happen.

FINAL QUESTIONS

I have some final questions for you.

- **Are you communicating positive messages to your employer?**
- **Are you communicating positive messages to your peers?**
- **Do you *want* to be promoted?**
- **Do you want to be seen as the right person for that amazing new opportunity—the person everyone is hoping gets the win?**

I also need to ask...

- **Are you communicating all of this through your energy, actions and behaviors and are you doing it consistently?**
- **Is there an opportunity to further elevate the quantity and quality of your interactions with others?**

I'll make this easy on you, the answer is always, YES!

There are over thirty ideas in this chapter designed to inspire immediate action. If you can embrace the concept of your personal ecosystem, and share the belief that your physical, emotional, and spiritual wellbeing influences your success—you will start seeing results immediately.

At its heart, *Rock Your Gig* is an anthem of excellence, it is calling us to take a new path, to reach ever higher with passionate focus and purposeful intent. The perspectives I have shared are what I believe to be the key contributors to my own career success. Beyond that, they are the central themes that brought crazy measures of fulfillment, joy, and happiness to my life. My hope is that they do the same for you.

Now, *Go Forth and Rock!*

– Rich McDonald

NOTES and RESOURCES

CHAPTER 1: THE SPIRIT OF REINVENTION

1. Pg. 21 – Kodak invented the world's first digital camera. kodak.com Milestones: https://www.kodak.com/US/en/corp/aboutus/heritage/milestones/default.htm. November 17, 2019.

2. Pg, 23 – Taiichi Ohno was a Japanese industrial engineer, recognized as one of the leaders in industrial engineering and designing the Toyota production system. Zhistory-biography.com. https://history-biography.com/taiichi-ohno/. November 17, 2019

CHAPTER 2: THE ECOSYSTEM OF "YOU"

3. Pg. 30 – Facts Over Time - Women In The Labor Force. US Department of Labor. https://www.dol.gov/wb/stats/NEWSTATS/facts/women_lf.htm#CivilianLFSex. November 17, 2019

4. Pg. 31 - United States Census Bureau - Income and Poverty In The United States: 2015. https://www.census.gov/library/publications/2016/demo/p60-256.html. November 19, 2019

5. Pg. 31 - CNBC - Here is how much debt American have at every age. https://www.cnbc.com/2018/08/20/how-much-debt-americans-have-at-every-age.html. October 28, 2019

6. Pg. 31 - Center For Disease Control and Prevention (CDC) Adult Obesity Facts. https://www.cdc.gov/obesity/data/adult.html. October 28, 2019

7. Pg. 31 – *The Matrix*. Dir. Andy Wachowski and Larry Wachowski. Warner Bros. Pictures, 1999. DVD.

8. Pg. 32 - Center For Disease Control and Prevention - *Opioid Overdose - Understanding the Epidemic*. https://www.cdc.gov/drugoverdose/epidemic/index.html. November, 18, 2019.

9. Pg. 33 - Natural News - *Nuremberg Trials: Big Pharma's Crimes Against Humanity*. https://www.naturalnews.com/024534_Europe_health_WHO.html. November 12, 2019

10. Pg. 33 – Today I Found Out - THE PHARMACEUTICAL COMPANY BAYER COINED THE NAME "HEROIN" AND MARKETED THE DRUG AS A NON-ADDICTIVE COUGH MEDICINE. http://www.todayifoundout.com/index.php/2012/02/the-pharmaceutical-company-bayer-coined-the-name-heroin-and-marketed-the-drug-as-a-non-addictive-cough-medicine/. November 21, 2019

CHAPTER 3: SITUATIONAL ANALYSIS

11. Pg.46 – Burn M.D., David D. (1980). *Feeling Good The New Mood Therapy*. New York, N.Y. : HarperCollins Publishing inc. pp. 28-43

12. Pg# TBD – *Think Up. Famous People That Have Succeeded Due to Affirmations and Positive Mindset*. https://thinkup.me/positive-mindset-affirmations/. November 21, 2019

13. Pg. 54 - The Mothers of Invention, Frank Zappa. "Discorporate and come with me" *Absolutely Free*, Verve Records,1967. Vinyl EP.

14. Pg. 58 – United Staes Census Bureau. Average One-Way Commuting Time by Metropolitan Areas. https://www.census.gov/library/visualizations/interactive/travel-time.html. August, 2019.

CHAPTER 6: PERSONALITY DESIGNS

15. Pg. 101 – Wolfe, Tom (1969). *The Electric Kool-Aid Acid Test* New York: Bantam.

16. Pg. 101 – Castaneda, Carlos (1971). *A Separate Reality* New York, N.Y: Simon and Schuster, inc.

17. Pg. 101 – Management Pocketbooks – David Merrill & Roger Reid: *Social Styles* https://www.pocketbook.co.uk/blog/2017/04/18/david-merrill-roger-reid-social-styles/. April, 2017. Posted by Mike Clayton.

CHAPTER 7: PERSONALITY DESIGN MÖBIUS

18. Pg. 109 - Wilson Learning (2004) - Social Styles Handbook. Nova Vista Publishing.

19. Pg. 110 – The Clash Mick Jones, *Should I Stay or Should I Go* Epic Records, 1979, Vinyl.

20. Pg. 113 – Queen, David Bowie, *Under Pressure* Hot Space.

EMI,1981, Vinyl.

CHAPTER 8: THE CONTROLLER

21. Pg. 119 - Schreiber, Flora Rheta (1973) *Sybil* Washington, D.C. Henry Regnery Company.

CHAPTER 8: THE CONNECTOR

22. Pg. 132 Emitt the Lego *The Lego Movie,*

CHAPTER 11: THE CALCULATOR

23. Pg. 141 – *2001: A Space Oddessy*, Stanley Kubrick. Metro-Goldwyn-Mayer (1968), film. Arthur C. Clarke, (1968) author Published by The New American Library, New York.

CHAPTER 12: METHODS AND TOOLS

24. Pg. 146 – Morrison, Terri and Conway, Wayne A. (2006) *Kiss Bow Or Shake Hands* New York, N.Y., Simon and Schuster, inc.

25. Pg. 147 – The British Library, Albert Mehrabian. https://www. bl.uk/people/albert-mehrabian. September, 2019

26. Pg. 164 – Fender®, Stratocaster® and Strat® are registered trademarks of Fender Musical Instruments Corporation.

CHAPTER 14: TENSION POINTS

27. Pg. 170 – George Thorogood and The Destroyers, *I Drink Alone* Maverick. EMI, 1985, Vinyl.

28. Pg, 171 – Mitch Hedberg, *Donut* https://www.youtube.com/ watch?v=EflOp6n6HPo. September, 2019.

29. Pg. 174 – Rush, *Free Will* Permanent Waves. Anthem /Mercury Records, 1980.